The Gravest Danger

THE GRAVEST DANGER

Nuclear Weapons

Sidney D. Drell
and
James E. Goodby

Foreword by
George P. Shultz

HOOVER INSTITUTION PRESS
Stanford University   Stanford, California

The Hoover Institution on War, Revolution and Peace,
founded at Stanford University in 1919 by Herbert Hoover,
who went on to become the thirty-first president of
the United States, is an interdisciplinary research center
for advanced study on domestic and international affairs.
The views expressed in its publications are entirely those of
the authors and do not necessarily reflect the views of the staff,
officers, or Board of Overseers of the Hoover Institution.

www.hoover.org

Hoover Institution Press Publication No. 524

Copyright © 2003 by the Board of Trustees of the
   Leland Stanford Junior University

First printing 2003
09   08   07   06   05   04   9   8   7   6   5   4   3   2

Manufactured in the United States of America

The paper used in this publication meets the minimum requirements
of American National Standard for Information Sciences—Permanence
of Paper for Printed Library Materials, ANSI Z39.48-1984. ⊗

Library of Congress Cataloging-in-Publication Data
Drell, Sidney D. (Sidney David), 1926–
   The gravest danger : nuclear weapons / Sidney D. Drell and
James E. Goodby.
          p.   cm.
   Includes index.
   ISBN 0-8179-4472-9 (alk. paper)
   1. Nuclear weapons.   2. Nuclear nonproliferation.   3. Nuclear
terrorism.   4. Nuclear disarmament.   5. World politics—21st
century.   I. Goodby, James E.   II. Title.
U264.D56 2003
327.1′747—dc22   2003061774

Contents

Foreword

AT THE DAWN of the nuclear age, Albert Einstein remarked, "Everything has changed but our way of thinking."

He was right for a time, but the devastating consequences of the use of a nuclear weapon did create a pattern of thinking that, with whatever flaws, served us well for half a century or so. Containment through deterrent capability worked. But the Cold War powers also realized that prevention was essential and that energetic efforts should be made to arrest the proliferation of nuclear weapons.

I well remember preparations for my first meeting as secretary of state with Soviet foreign minister Gromyko in September 1982. I had assumed office in July. The temperature of the Cold War was frigid, the atmosphere confrontational, and I was counseled to act accordingly. I said, "OK, but there must be something we can do to identify a mutual interest."

There were to be two meetings, held about a week apart. I got the president's authorization to suggest, at the end of the first meeting, a few topics on which we might try to work collaboratively. Nuclear nonproliferation was one of them. Toward the end of the second meeting, Gromyko replied to my suggestions, expressing a willingness to make open and joint efforts to avoid the proliferation of nuclear weapons. So, even at the height of the Cold War, we were hard at work on our way of thinking.

The subject took high priority on Ronald Reagan's agenda. He thought that "mutual assured destruction" was not only MAD but also was an essentially immoral way to keep the peace. He said repeatedly, "A nuclear war cannot be won and must never be fought." His aim was to abolish nuclear weapons. However elusive that goal may have been, he did start the ball rolling toward reduction in the Soviet and U.S. arsenals. But he worried, prophetically, about rogue states obtaining even one of these awesome weapons.

Clearly, the end of the Cold War has drastically reduced the threat of nuclear holocaust. But the world remains a dangerous place in different ways. In a world of terrorist threats and rogues that call themselves states yet behave outside the bounds of civilized norms, we are once again called upon to examine our concepts. That is what this book is about, and no intellectual task is more urgent or more relevant to current operational issues.

Sid Drell and Jim Goodby have between them vast experience in the area of nuclear weapons and have long been active voices in the nuclear debate. In this volume, they put their key recommendations right up front, in their introduction. That is appropriate. The reader knows at the outset where the authors are going. All of their conclusions have deep merit and the weight of careful argument and factual development. Some will be the subject of debate. That debate, in turn, is one of the important purposes of this book.

Having had the privilege of reading this work in earlier manuscript form and discussing its subject at length with the authors, I value this book because of its essence: the careful development of a framework for thinking about nuclear weapons in times punctuated by terrorist threats.

All the elements are here: a relevant history, including an illuminating chart on page 6 on the time pattern of state acquisition of nuclear weapons; a virtual inventory of preventive actions; a searching examination of the circumstances when preemptive military action may be necessary; the problems of intelligence and monitoring; a new look at ballistic missile defenses; the importance of the U.S. example (as in testing); and ideas about what Russia and the United States can do with their special responsibilities. The authors develop the necessary interplay of strength and diplomacy as they address current problems. Work your way through the issues that are presented in settings in various countries. You will find, as I have, that the analytic framework will help you develop your own ideas of how to address critical problems.

Now is a time that cries out for new concepts, often using old principles, about how the world works. If he were still around, Einstein might well be challenging us once again to examine "our way of thinking." And in doing so, he would surely find in Drell and Goodby worthy partners as they address the gravest danger.

George P. Shultz
September 2003

Preface

THE TWO OF us have worked together, on and off, for more than twenty years on national security issues, both in public and in private capacities. We have long been convinced that nuclear weapons, whether in the hands of friendly or hostile states, pose a mortal danger to humanity. This danger is unique in its terrifying potential for devastation on an unprecedented and unimaginable scale. Nothing else compares with it. We agree with President George W. Bush's assessment that the nexus of radicalism and weapons of mass destruction is where the gravest dangers to our nation lie, and where the international community must act as one to head off these dangers.

The public debate about this threat needs, in our view, a comprehensive review of the main policy issues and their related implications. We found none that we thought meets the needs of the public. Therefore, we set out in this book to provide one, calling on our respective professional backgrounds, one scientific and one diplomatic.

Our aim has been to follow a strategic approach: to identify a broad, long-term goal and to analyze the means available to reach that goal. Recognizing that policy recommendations have their ultimate test in how those ideas fit the real-world situations, we applied our strategic approach to specific countries: those that are critically important to the success of an anti-proliferation policy. These include, in addition to the United States, the established nuclear weapon states of Russia and China, the de facto nuclear weapon states, India and Pakistan, and the undeclared or potential nuclear states: Israel, Iran, and North Korea. We assumed that Great Britain and France, both well-established nuclear weapon states, would broadly agree with our analysis and policy prescriptions, although that remains to be seen since both have been relatively silent on these issues.

Our basic conclusion is that the United States can and must provide strong leadership to rebuild an international framework to strengthen the non-proliferation regime and preserve the existing norm against the use of nuclear weapons. American and allied diplomacy, complemented by credible force, built a bulwark against nuclear proliferation and the use of nuclear weapons through the darkest years of the Cold War. This gives reason for optimism to think that success can be ours today against the new threats posed by rogue nations and terrorism. By its very nature this effort requires worldwide cooperation and determined leadership by the United States.

We see this book as a contribution to public discussion on such matters as the role of targeted diplomacy backed by military force in combating nuclear proliferation, and the impact of U.S. nuclear weapons policies on proliferation decisions by other nations. Our intent has been to sketch out the argument briefly and in terms accessible to the general public. We hope that our book will stimulate an active public dialogue. Reducing nuclear danger and preventing nuclear conflict is a major challenge for the United States and all other nations in the world.

Sidney D. Drell
James E. Goodby

Acknowledgments

EARLY DRAFTS OF this manuscript were read by David Holloway, Wolfgang Panofsky, Harry Rowen, and George Shultz. We wish to recognize and thank them for their important criticisms and for valuable discussions on the issues addressed in this book, from which it—and we— have benefited greatly. S.D. wishes to express his appreciation to the Hoover Institution and its director, John Raisian, for their continuing support. J.G. wishes to express his thanks to the Institute of International Studies at Stanford and its director, David Holloway, for their support of this project carried out in the winter and early spring of 2003 during which time J.G. was the Diplomat-in-Residence at Stanford University's Institute of International Studies. We also wish to thank Bonnie Rose for efficient and essential help in preparing the manuscript, and Patricia Baker, the Executive Editor, and her staff at Hoover Institution Press for their excellent support in turning our manuscript into this book. Finally, we wish to acknowledge Petrus Buwalda, Pierce Corden, Nancy Gallagher, Richard Garwin, Hon. Lee Hamilton, Raymond Jeanloz, Ted Postol, Larry Scheinman, and Strobe Talbott for their encouragement and many useful comments. Responsibility for the book's contents, of course, falls only on the shoulders of the authors.

Introduction:
The Nuclear Danger

"THE CROSSROADS OF radicalism and technology," said President George W. Bush, is the locus of "the gravest danger our nation faces." He was speaking of the acquisition of weapons of mass destruction—nuclear, chemical, biological, and radiological—by rogue states or terrorist groups. Any of these types of weapons would be a serious threat in the hands of those bent on causing enormous damage to achieve their ends. But nuclear weapons, as measured by their destructive potential, surely present the gravest danger.

Biological agents may ultimately come to rival nuclear weapons as a threat to the whole population but for now they should be feared primarily for their potential for creating havoc and terror. Chemical weapons already can kill on a large scale, but "mass destruction" is not the term that accurately describes their lethality. Civil defense and advanced medical techniques could potentially become very effective in mitigating the consequences of chemical and biological agents. Nuclear weapons, on the other hand, are so destructive that there is no practical way to make the consequences of their use more bearable for civilian populations.

These weapons are unique in their terrifying potential for massive destruction on an unprecedented and unimaginable scale. With them, for the first time in history mankind has the capacity to threaten human survival.

Father Bryan Hehir, former dean of Harvard Divinity School, observed in a keynote address on "Ethical Considerations of Living in the Nuclear Age" at a Stanford University conference in 1987:

> For millennia people believed that if anyone had the right to call the ultimate moment of truth, one must name that person God. Since the dawn of the nuclear age we have progressively acquired the capacity to call the ultimate moment of truth and we are not gods. But we must live with what we have created.

To avoid nuclear war and to contain and gradually to diminish the potential for nuclear devastation: these are the most compelling imperatives of our time. George Tenet, Director of Central Intelligence, has cautioned, however, that we are seeing "the continuing weakening of the international non-proliferation consensus," and "the domino theory of the 21st century may well be nuclear." Absent a vigorous diplomatic effort to prevent it, that prediction may turn out to be on the mark. India and Pakistan with help from abroad have developed and tested nuclear weapons but each is now regarded as a partner of the United States in the fight against terrorism. North Korea has withdrawn from the non-proliferation treaty and evicted inspectors from the International Atomic Energy Agency. The administration has rightly said that North Korea is a regional problem which it is now addressing as events move to a critical stage. Iran is proceeding to build the infrastructure for a nuclear weapons program. The treaty that would ban all tests of nuclear weapons remains unratified. A protocol that would strengthen the inspection authority of the International Atomic Energy Agency has yet to be acted upon by many nations. Israel's undeclared nuclear weapons arsenal is untouched by any anti-proliferation effort in the Middle East.

The top priority of the United States, and of other leading nations, should be to strengthen the international nonproliferation consensus. Preventing nuclear proliferation is far preferable to dealing with its consequences. Some of the weakening of the global consensus is U.S.-inspired. Not only is the reluctance of the United States to ratify the Comprehensive Test Ban Treaty a serious blow to the nuclear Non-Proliferation Treaty, but strategic doctrines issued by the administration in 2002 have also raised serious questions and concerns. Much of the weakening, however, stems from a perception in several countries, particularly in Asia after the end of the bipolar order of the Cold War, that in a dangerous world nuclear weapons are essential for national security, and in addition contribute to prestige. The United States needs to reinvigorate its anti-proliferation policy, now increasingly viewed as selective in its application and as overly reliant on military force, an instrument that is mostly unusable, and only temporarily effective at best.

The nuclear genie cannot be put back in the bottle. It is a noble thing to strive for a world that achieves such human perfection that the complete elimination of nuclear weapons would be more than a distant dream, but that will not happen until a day that is far beyond the horizon of the most ambitious plans of the world's visionaries. For the foreseeable future the most urgent task is to successfully manage, contain, and reduce this gravest danger that our nation faces—nuclear weapons, whether in the hands of adversaries or of friendly states.

Good progress was being made until recently. With sustained effort, creative diplomacy, some wisdom, and a good measure of luck, the community of nations has, over the fifty-eight years since Hiroshima and Nagasaki, imprinted powerful traditions of non-use and non-possession of nuclear weapons on national behavior. Those norms have been challenged recently by India, Pakistan, Iraq, Iran, and North Korea. Others may not be far behind. The use of nuclear weapons in combat is becoming a plausible near-term possibility. The non-proliferation regime has also been threatened by the spread of weapons technology to more and more parts of the world. These advances are empowering people of evil intent, of which there is no shortage, by giving them ever more devastating means for destruction. Some of these people may be suicidal terrorists who view their cause as justifying any and all means, no matter how deadly and repugnant.

Governments that are responsible and well-intentioned by any fair standard also are being forced to consider something that previously had been unthinkable: whether to acquire nuclear weapons. This is particularly a problem in Asia, where the telltale signs of an incipient nuclear arms race already can be seen. If the international anti-proliferation consensus becomes seriously eroded, some nations that have relied on the U.S. nuclear umbrella may have to consider acquiring their own nuclear weapons. Even though such developments might not affect U.S. national security directly, they would doom the efforts of anti-proliferation policies to prevent the spread of nuclear weapons, to discourage the use of these weapons, and to roll back current programs. Ultimately, the Non-Proliferation Treaty would become a dead letter.

Recent events are discouraging and troubling, but there is still room for hope if the United States exerts its leadership with wisdom and patience.

Amidst the new challenges posed by terrorism and by the nexus of radicalism and technology, it is all too easy to forget the major successes achieved in containing the nuclear danger through patient diplomacy, including the coercive use of diplomacy. Preventive war was suggested in the 1950s when the Soviet Union, and in the 1960s when China, began to build their nuclear arsenals. But by the early years of the twenty-first century committed state-craft had created a world where most nations were overwhelmingly united in the quest to prevent proliferation of nuclear weapons.

Today, as shown in Figure 1, only eight nations are confirmed nuclear weapon states: the United States, the United Kingdom, Russia, China, and France, who have signed the Non-Proliferation Treaty; India and Pakistan who tested nuclear weapons designs five years ago; and Israel, a non-declared nuclear weapon state. The evidence is unclear as regards North Korea, even though North Korea's government wishes the world to believe it has them. This number is far smaller than was anticipated when the Non-Proliferation Treaty entered into force in 1970.

This slow pace of proliferation during the decades since Hiroshima and Nagasaki is all the more impressive when one adds up the number of nations that contemplated and, in some cases, actually started down the path to building nuclear weapons before abandoning them. And there are a number of other nations who, after flirting with the idea of acquiring nuclear weapons, realized that

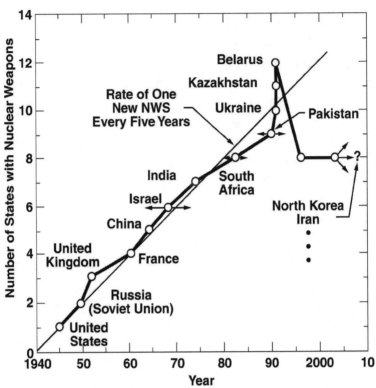

Figure 1   Number of states with nuclear weapons, by year, from 1945 to the present. South Africa, Belarus, Kazakhstan, and Ukraine disposed of their in the 1990s.

their security and the stability of the world were better served by their joining in developing a non-proliferation regime rather than a national nuclear force.

At present, all but four of the world's nations—India, Israel, Pakistan, plus North Korea which recently withdrew—have signed on to the indefinite extension of the nuclear Non-Proliferation Treaty. This record provides a strong basis for being optimistic about the continued success of patient diplomacy, creatively and aggressively

applied by the United States in partnership with like-
minded nations.

The recent efforts of North Korea, Iran, and Iraq to
build the basis for nuclear weapons programs have also
taught us two lessons. One is that covert efforts may be
successful temporarily in hiding the full extent of these
programs, as in Iraq in the 1980s, and more recently in
Iran and North Korea with respect to their uranium
enrichment programs. But these programs did not evade
detection for long. The same holds true for Israel, India,
and Pakistan. The other lesson is that unless nuclear proliferation issues are addressed as integral parts of the
broad security context in which these issues arise, proliferant countries sooner or later will try to slip out of any
constraints that temporarily limit their nuclear ambitions.
That was the case in North Korea and probably in Iraq as
well. It is likely to be the case in Iran.

This book addresses actions and policies that the community of nations—with American leadership—should
take to confront and turn back the nuclear danger that
imperils humanity. Some of the actions and policies that
will be presented and defended in this book are as follows:

- Waging a long-term campaign against nuclear proliferation is essential for the security of the United States
  and other nations. Losing that struggle would change
  the daily lives of ordinary citizens and accentuate the
  kinds of instabilities that were felt in the aftermath of
  9/11. The use of nuclear weapons in war might become
  commonplace and endanger civilization.

- So far, the battle to contain and roll back the number
  of nuclear weapon states has been successful. Several

nations have renounced nuclear weapons and only eight now possess them. The prospects are good that we can do at least as well in the next fifty years if the United States, in partnership with other major powers, adopts comprehensive rollback policies.

- Pre-emption to destroy an impending strike with nuclear weapons is an entirely justifiable action, but it requires exquisite intelligence and public understanding.

- Preventive war to forestall a nuclear threat that is potential but not yet imminent is the policy that the administration has adopted and used as a major factor in the case of Iraq. The occasions for exercising that policy are likely to be quite limited.

- A range of policies and programs designed to deny access to nuclear weapons to nations and sub-state entities have been employed and, to a degree, have worked. These include export controls, which need to be more uniformly applied. Cooperative threat reduction (the Nunn-Lugar program) has been successful but needs much more resources and improved cooperation in efforts to remove impediments to progress. Ballistic missile defense, designed to dissuade states from acquiring nuclear weapons or to blunt an attack if dissuasion fails, is expected to be of limited value. Intelligence is critical, and needs to be strengthened.

- International organizations can help in the campaign, especially the International Atomic Energy Agency (IAEA), and the United Nations Security Council (UNSC) in an enforcement role. The inspection mandate of the IAEA needs to be strengthened as soon as possible. The UNSC also needs greater help from the IAEA in combating nuclear terrorism.

- The two states possessing more than 90 percent of the nuclear weapons of the world—the United States and Russia—have unfinished business left over from the Cold War. The Bush-Putin Declaration of Moscow in May 2002 had an excellent agenda for completing that business but it is languishing, unimplemented. That situation must be changed.

- China and the United States need to engage more systematically on nuclear issues. One tool that would help would be a bilateral Consultative Commission at the ministerial level.

- The administration favors a "targeted strategy" to deal with specific nations considered potential proliferants. The idea is sound but should encompass cooperation, as well as confrontation, and should view the problem in the context of the strategic circumstances that motivated decisions to develop nuclear weapons.

- Although some Americans expect other nations to follow the U.S. lead in matters of war and peace (and are surprised if they do not), these same Americans argue that what Washington says and does about nuclear weapons has no effect on other countries. Of course, the dynamics of military interaction works today as it has in the past: If the United States places more reliance on nuclear weapons, other nations will too. U.S. policies need to be carefully reviewed for their potential impact abroad.

- Since 1945 restraint in nuclear affairs has played an

important role in preventing the use of nuclear weapons in war. It has helped to limit the number of nuclear weapon states to eight. The Non-Proliferation Treaty must be bolstered with other actions. These include U.S. reductions in nuclear weapons; continuing the non-use tradition; reducing the salience of nuclear weapons in the U.S. military strategy; continuing the moratorium on underground tests of nuclear weapons and ratifying the Comprehensive Test Ban Treaty (CTBT).

• The threat posed by nuclear proliferation requires new forms of defense cooperation on a multilateral basis. A multilateral ballistic missile early warning system and a cooperative effort to develop a ballistic missile defense would help to build a stronger anti-proliferation coalition. Cooperative threat reduction also should be made a global program.

I. From the Past to the Present

Was the Past a Precedent or an Exception?

In revulsion at the wanton, indiscriminate loss of human life that use of chemical and biological weapons can inflict, and dubious about the military utility of these weapons, nations have agreed to forgo their possession and use. These norms of non-possession and non-use are broadly endorsed and honored by most nations, but some honor them only in the breach, especially as regards enforcement. Evidently such formal agreements or treaties, while necessary to establish standards of behavior, alone are not sufficient to ensure full compliance.

The treatment of nuclear weapons has been different. These weapons have not been outlawed and their use has not been prohibited. Tens of thousands of nuclear weapons exist, and some nations, including the United States and Russia, have declared that they feel free to use them to meet a serious attack, whether nuclear or not. This is not a reflection of indifference about their destructive potential. It has happened because, almost from their inception, nuclear weapons formed the central pillar of the bipolar structure of the Cold War. Seeing this, non-nuclear weapon states concluded that the non-proliferation regime was inherently discriminatory; naturally they pressed the five original nuclear powers—the United States, the Soviet Union (now Russia), the United Kingdom, France, and China—to reduce their nuclear arsenals and their reliance on these weapons.

The Soviet Union and the United States, over the years of their bitter competition, each built many thousands of nuclear weapons and mated them with the most advanced means of delivery that they could devise. The number of nuclear weapons grew rapidly during the 1970s as new technologies led to the deployment of multiple highly accurate warheads on individual missiles (MIRVs). This trend was reversed in the late 1980s by the landmark agreement between President Ronald Reagan and Soviet President Mikhail Gorbachev to eliminate intermediate-range ballistic and ground-launched cruise missiles, and to advance the negotiations that led to START I, both of which are still in effect. But despite this, nuclear weapons remained of central importance in the war preparations of Moscow and Washington, and remain so today. War planning in the United States included repeated nuclear strikes as part of a doctrine of "protracted nuclear war," endorsed by President Jimmy Carter. Similarly the Soviets wrote about war-fighting and war-winning nuclear use doctrines. Throughout the nuclear era, however, elaborate measures were taken on both sides to ensure that nuclear weapons would not be used except under the direst of circumstances and only as directed by the heads of government and top military commanders. Many of these measures were administrative assignments of authority and procedures to assure positive control. Others were technical or physical features that would prevent unauthorized persons from gaining access to nuclear weapons or from detonating them if they did. Some were in the military or intelligence fields, ensuring the accuracy of information about the actions and intentions of the adversary and avoiding direct military combat at any level.

The Soviet Union and the United States followed these and other procedures independently of the other but not completely autonomously. There was an awareness of what the other was doing; certain expectations developed on each side about the proper control of nuclear weapons. This system of parallel restraint broke down only once in a way that threatened war—the Cuban missile crisis of 1962. A notable example of parallel unilateral measures was the decision by President George H. W. Bush in 1989 to withdraw U.S. tactical nuclear weapons from forward deployment, shortly thereafter reciprocated by President Gorbachev for the Soviet Union.

The United States and the Soviet Union also sought to regulate their bilateral nuclear competition through treaties. Those agreements formalized the idea that relations between heavily armed adversaries could be cooperative, as well as competitive. Even though these treaties were accompanied by occasional real and alleged violations, they provided valuable predictability, reinforced parallel practices, and heightened the two nations' awareness of each other's military thinking. It is not at all clear that the kind of feedback loop that existed between the United States and the Soviet Union will inform the actions of other interacting nuclear weapon states. Of course, the leaders of India and Pakistan understand very well the principles of strategic stability. In fact, they have declared explicitly that they will follow them. But the deep hostility between them has so far prevented the kind of adversarial cooperation that makes effective arms control possible. The same can be expected in other regions.

The Soviet Union and the United States also worked together to shape the global nuclear environment in which their competition took place. Their efforts were generally, although not always, aimed at preventing nuclear proliferation. Nothing like that is happening in the case of India, Pakistan, and China and would be most unlikely to happen in the case of North Korea and Iran. The United States and the Soviet Union each created alliances that had the effect of extending nuclear deterrence to other countries. In the case of American alliances, both in Europe and in Northeast Asia, governments that might have decided to build nuclear weapons relied on the U.S. nuclear deterrent instead of their own. The United States and the Soviet Union cooperated to slow down or prevent the acquisition of nuclear weapons by third countries. They did this through treaties open to all nations, such as the limited nuclear test ban treaty and the nuclear Non-Proliferation Treaty. They also collaborated in denying technology and nuclear materials through their own national export controls and through guidelines developed with other nations. When the Soviet Union collapsed, Russia and the United States cooperated in securing the return to Russia of nuclear weapons that had been deployed in Belarus, Kazakhstan, and Ukraine.

In contrast to this, the acquisition of nuclear weapons by India and Pakistan has weakened the non-proliferation regime. If North Korea proceeds to develop and deploy a substantial nuclear weapons arsenal, this will push even an anti-nuclear Japan to give serious thought to becoming a nuclear weapon state. Responsible and law-abiding governments like those of South Korea and Taiwan may have to follow suit. An Asian nuclear arms race could ensue.

The restraint regime eventually constructed by the nuclear superpowers during the Cold War is not necessarily going to be replicated in this phase of the nuclear era.

The most important achievement of Moscow and Washington was to establish a norm: nuclear weapons were not to be used. At no time did the two governments sign a treaty or issue a statement saying this. Their strategic doctrines rested on the proposition that nuclear weapons could be used. From time to time, dangerous forms of nuclear diplomacy were employed by the two countries, in particular by Soviet General Secretary Nikita Khrushchev and U.S. President Richard Nixon. But to this day, nuclear weapons were never used. Nearly sixty years of non-use certainly established a precedent. Nuclear weapons, as NATO's official doctrine has proclaimed, have become weapons of last resort. This precedent— without a doubt the most important precedent of the Cold War—is now in some danger. It is jeopardized by the possible acquisition of nuclear weapons by terrorist organizations and the spread of nuclear weapons to countries that occasionally engage in hot wars with one another. The prospects of more nuclear weapon states around the rim of Asia, heightened tensions in Northeast Asia and South Asia, and continuing hostilities in the Middle East pose urgent threats to international peace and security.

U.S. Policies

The established norm of non-use of nuclear weapons also has been challenged by recent policy statements by the Bush administration concerning the roles and missions of U.S. nuclear forces. The assertion has been made that a nuclear response to the use of biological weapons in combat would be appropriate. There is also a tendency in U.S. official circles to consider the use of low-yield nuclear weapons against deep underground hardened bunkers a reasonable option in a limited war. And deterrence is considered to be enhanced on the grounds that use of such low-yield nuclear weapons would be approved by U.S. national command authorities, or at least potential adversaries might believe that to be so. Such a policy would be in direct conflict with the tacit understanding that gradually emerged as the world moved through the first fifty-eight years of the nuclear age: the only rational purpose for nuclear weapons is to deter the use of nuclear weapons by an opponent and to respond in kind if attacked with nuclear weapons.

Deterrence emerged as the key concept of the nuclear age when the terrifying consequences of nuclear war became generally known and were confronted by the human conscience for the first time. Nuclear bombs were not just one more weapon. With an energy release a million times larger than that of weapons previously known to mankind, mass destruction is inevitable. No protection is possible. These weapons present humanity with a fundamental issue: can civilization survive? "We are rapidly getting to the point that no war can be won," said President Dwight Eisenhower in 1956. Conventional wars can be fought to exhaustion and surrender, but nuclear war can come close to "destruction of the enemy *and* suicide." Ronald Reagan understood this in his bones and, while in office, often said, "A nuclear war cannot be won and must never be fought." These facts make it imperative for the United States to reaffirm that the singular purpose of its nuclear weapons is to avoid their use, not only by others against the United States and its allies but also by the United States against anyone else. The United States must prepare to meet its vital interests in the world by developing and training twenty-first century conventional forces against emerging threats, while pursuing diplomacy to discourage, if not prevent, the development of threats posed by nuclear weapons.

The United States should leave no doubt about its intentions to take action preemptively if it perceives an imminent threat of the use of biological or chemical weapons, and to respond forcefully against any actual use of biological or chemical weapons in combat. The threat to try commanders for war crimes if Iraq used any of these weapons was entirely correct and a deterrent in itself. At the same time, the technical realities of nuclear weapons and their effects must be recognized and their value in confronting biological and chemical weapons or hardened deeply buried targets should not be exaggerated. This point will be discussed more fully later but these technical factors are relevant:

- It is impossible to destroy hardened underground bunkers or military targets with a nuclear bomb without generating a substantial cloud of deadly radioactivity.

- The effective range of nuclear weapons in neutralizing the deadly effects of biological pathogens and chemical gases is severely limited by the fact that the blast effects of nuclear weapons extend beyond the range of the high temperatures and radiation they create when detonated underground, and that are required for destroying such agents.

- A great payoff in the ability of military systems to destroy hardened underground targets can be gained from improvements in intelligence that make it possible to locate, identify, and characterize such targets with accuracy, and to define and identify their vulnerable points such as tunnel entrances or air ducts.

- Additional gains could be achieved by improving the ability of weapons with hardened reentry bodies and armed with conventional explosives to penetrate into the earth to depths of several tens of feet or more before detonating, thereby delivering a significantly larger shock onto the target than if they were detonated at or near the surface.

If the United States, the strongest nation in the world, concludes that it cannot protect its vital interests without relying on nuclear weapons in limited war situations, whether against biological weapons or deeply buried targets, it would be a clear signal to other nations that nuclear weapons are necessary for their security purposes. That inevitably would dash any hope of reducing nuclear danger by strengthening a non-proliferation regime. Diplomatic operations, in the context of a policy of defensive last resort for nuclear weapons, offer the best hope for preserving and strengthening a non-proliferation regime in the years ahead.

Emerging U.S.-Russian Relations

The collapse of the Soviet Union, the end of the Cold War, and the transformation of the United States–Soviet/Russian relationship have radically changed the way in which the nuclear threat is perceived by the two nations, and by others. In some ways the danger appears to have receded: deep crises in the American-Russian relationship are not likely to occur. In the past, it was not implausible to think that a U.S.-Soviet nuclear war might be triggered by tensions over access to Berlin, conflicts in the Middle East, or Soviet deployment of missiles in Cuba. Operations of nuclear-equipped sea and air units of the two sides, especially in times of tension, generated additional worries about the adversary's intentions. The deployment of new strategic weapons systems, indeed almost any action that seemed to threaten the military balance, injected fresh concerns into the already troubled relationship. All that is gone, probably forever.

But the perception, both in America and in Russia, that the other is not fully to be trusted in the life-or-death matter of nuclear weaponry has not completely disappeared. Thus, the United States deems it necessary to hold in reserve thousands of warheads as a hedge against a renewal of hostility between the two countries. Russia does not fully trust U.S. assurances that the American ballistic missile defense system is not directed at gaining a decisive advantage in the nuclear relationship. It is a further cause for serious concern that both nations have kept their nuclear forces on high alert, ready to launch on very short notice. The existence of the other's nuclear-armed ballistic missiles is the only conceivable threat that would justify this. And so neither Russia nor the United States really has moved beyond a peace that is conditional.

The nuclear danger posed by this state of affairs is latent, hardly noticed on a day-to-day basis except by those manning the nuclear ramparts on each side, but it

limits what the two nations can do together. The legacy of
the Cold War still shadows the relationship.

This legacy is felt in other, more direct ways as well.
The Ministry of Atomic Energy (MINATOM) was a state
within the state during Soviet times. Whole cities were part
of its domain and a sizable portion of the Soviet work force
was employed in one way or another by the Ministry.
MINATOM is still a force to be reckoned with in the new
Russia. Its potential as a hard currency earner gives it a
certain independence, even in foreign affairs. Its dealings
with Iran, for example, have been a major source of irri-
tation between Washington and Moscow. U.S.-Russian
collaboration in nuclear non-proliferation has been ham-
pered by MINATOM's determination to sustain its industrial and technological base through contacts and
contracts with other countries that are, at best, questionable in terms of blocking the spread of nuclear weapons
to additional nations. The new relationship between Russia and the United States should permit a greater common
understanding between the two countries regarding per-
missible exports under Article IV of the nuclear Non-Proliferation Treaty. This has not yet been achieved; the
problem deserves a higher priority.

Another legacy of the Cold War is the large quantity of
nuclear materials and nuclear warheads stored in less
than ideal security circumstances. With the lifting of the
oppressive measures that regulated travel and other
aspects of life in the Soviet Union, and the deterioration of
Russian security services, there came a need for new systems of protecting and accounting for nuclear materials.
Substantial progress has been made in installing new systems, but vulnerabilities remain. A market exists for

nuclear weapons–usable materials which Russia may inadvertently supply unless these vulnerabilities are eliminated.

An example of successful U.S. statecraft deployed to deal with this problem is the Nunn-Lugar Cooperative Threat Reduction program. Funded by the United States Congress since 1992, the program provides, *inter alia*, for material protection, control, and accountability (MPC&A) of the special nuclear material (plutonium 239, and enriched uranium) in the former Soviet Union. The largest stockpiles of the world's nuclear weapons and fuel reside there. As reported in 2002 by the Harvard University Project on Managing the Atom (Matthew Bunn, John P. Holdren, and Anthony Weir, 2002), Russia still has some 160 tons of separated plutonium and 1,100 tons of highly enriched uranium, enough fuel for more than 50,000 nuclear warheads, in addition to its approximately 20,000 warheads that already exist. Material is reportedly spread across more than 250 buildings at 50 sites. Warheads are located in more than 60 sites, in more than 160 storage bunkers. This constitutes a very rich treasure for would-be proliferators or terrorists, emphasizing the importance of cooperative measures to secure them from theft or sale.

This situation speaks to the continuing need for U.S.-Russian cooperation to tame the nuclear danger that hangs over the world:

• First, the two nations need to work at escaping from the mutual nuclear deterrence trap that still continues to ensnare them; their relations should become more like those that the United States has with Britain and France.

- Second, the two nations need to work more closely together in denying potential proliferant countries access to nuclear materials.

- Third, Russia and America need to be especially vigilant regarding the half-century-old de facto prohibition on the use of nuclear weapons in war.

A Nuclear Nightmare

Although vitally important work remains to be done with Russia, the nuclear threat has changed significantly since the Cold War ended. Several states in regions afflicted by persisting national rivalries and disputes have either acquired nuclear weapons or are building the basis for acquiring nuclear weapons in the future. India and Pakistan have a territorial dispute that is at the top of each country's agenda, and each has now acquired nuclear weapons. This has not calmed the situation. Indeed, it can be argued that, with both nations now having nuclear capabilities, Pakistan was enabled to conduct a war of infiltration against India and to support terrorist activities in Kashmir without fear of a major Indian military response, precisely because both nations possess nuclear weapons. If non-nuclear-use guidelines exist at all in the subcontinent, there is no reason to think that they will be long lasting. The comparison of India and Pakistan today to the United States and the Soviet Union during the Cold War is not valid: the two superpowers were not neighbors and had no territorial disputes; their armed conflicts were never with each other. A large-scale Indian invasion of Pakistan in the name of cauterizing the bleeding wound of Kashmir would test a non-nuclear-use rule to the utmost. And neither side thinks that that scenario is out of the question. Furthermore, it seems clear that New Delhi and Islamabad are each aiming some of their public policy statements at Washington, in an effort to get the United States to pressure the other side. The presence of the United States as a third party introduces a complexity not seen in the U.S.–Soviet Union confrontation and adds another layer of unpredictability. It also puts a heavy burden on the United States to judge the situation correctly.

Iran may have no present intentions to build nuclear weapons, as it claims, but it is certainly putting itself in a position to build them in the future. Seeing itself as a potential victim of several hostile nations, the United States included, Iran probably conceives of nuclear weapons as a deterrent and as a means of gaining regional prestige and strategic leverage. Saddam Hussein's nuclear weapons program must have influenced thinking in Tehran. Conversely, whatever the rationale, an Iranian atomic bomb would have some effect on future Iraqi defense planning, no matter who controls that nation in the years to come. Israel would be bound to view a nuclear-armed Iran as yet another serious threat to its survival.

North Korea's acquisition of a declared and increasingly robust nuclear weapons stockpile would make it all but certain that Japan and South Korea also would build nuclear weapons. Taiwan might not be far behind, a possibility that probably would bring a preemptive attack by China to the forefront of international concerns. Very likely the prospect of such destabilizing developments is stimulating efforts by the Chinese to stop the North Korean program.

These developments all around the rim of Asia are

setting the stage for the next chapter in the history of the nuclear age. The plot of this story is shaping up already:

- The era of managed nuclear weapons competition, essentially by two nations, is over;

- the predictability that Moscow and Washington tried, with some success, to build into the system will give way to increasing uncertainty and worst-case assumptions;

- proliferation of nuclear weapons capabilities will proceed at a near-geometrical rate as new nuclear weapon states over time beget more than one imitator;

- the stability fostered by a long period of non-proliferation will break down as political and other restraints prove unable to stem the tide;

- this will generate increased pressures on many countries in unstable regions to make biological weapons to offset growing nuclear capabilities around them;

- transnational terrorist organizations will have an easier time gaining access to nuclear weapons owing to loss of control over these weapons by unstable governments, or even by deliberate transfer of the weapons;

- this cascade of easily foreseeable events will lead, sooner or later, to the use of nuclear weapons in combat by nation-states, or to attacks on major population centers by terrorists equipped with nuclear weapons;

- the taboo against the use of nuclear weapons will erode to the point where preventive war will seem to be the safest course for those nations capable of it.

Containment and Deterrence

This nightmare scenario is itself based on worst-case assumptions, it may be argued: will not the deterrent effect of nuclear weapons demonstrated in the U.S.-Soviet competition be the overwhelming consequence of nuclear proliferation, as Kenneth Waltz maintains in his book, *The Spread of Nuclear Weapons: A Debate Renewed*, with Scott D. Sagan (W. W. Norton, 2003); why should control of these weapons not be as effective as it has been in the past?

Scott Sagan, in the same book, has described, in convincing detail, a number of frightening incidents involving U.S. nuclear weapons resulting from the failure of command and control and from flaws in the management of nuclear weapons—incidents that occurred even though those in charge of nuclear weapons paid a great deal of attention to safety and security. He suggests that expectations of an impeccable performance by newly minted nuclear powers are misplaced.

The main interest of both the Soviet Union and the United States during the Cold War was in maintaining the status quo in Europe. Europe was the only place where an all-out nuclear conflict between them would have been almost automatic if a war had broken out, certainly in the early stages of the Cold War. Cuba and the Middle East generated nuclear crises that resulted from mistakes or miscalculations but these were contained. A similar mistake in Berlin would have been catastrophic. With the consolidation of clear-cut spheres of interest in Europe, and a growing recognition, in both Moscow and Washington, of war's calamitous consequences, the likelihood of nuclear war had dropped, almost to the vanishing point, by the time the Cold War ended. Both sides were satisfied with the status quo. But the status quo is not an objective that is commonly accepted in regions where future arms races may occur—not in the Middle East, not in South Asia, and not in East Asia. The calming effect of being satisfied with things as they are will not be there to restrain the prime antagonists.

Despite this, containment and deterrence will have their role to play in relations between nation-states for a very long time to come, although of course there are limits beyond which the behavior of governments of any stripe cannot be influenced. To act in a manner that suggests those two concepts have lost their value in inter-state relations would be to cast aside two extremely useful tools of foreign policy. The consequences could be extremely damaging—for the United States and for others.

Deterrence presupposes that the threat of certain destruction of an enemy will induce prudence in that nation's policies. In the absence of that expectation and that effect, inter-state relations would truly become, in the words of Thomas Hobbes, "a war of all against all." Much of the fabric of international cooperation has been stitched together by attempts to make the world safe for deterrence, in the belief that living in the nuclear age implies a willingness to think of force as a last resort and that rules should be constructed to encourage that outcome. Terrorists have tried to change that rule by challenging Churchill's views about the effect of nuclear deterrence: "By a sublime irony of fate, safety will be the sturdy child of terror, and survival the twin brother of annihilation." Churchill was thinking of the impending struggle between the West and the Soviet Union, and that time is past. But modern weapons of any type should exert a powerful effect on rational decision-makers when they consider war or peace issues.

The terrorists have almost succeeded in convincing some people that deterrence will not work, even against nation-states, and that preventive war is the only meaningful strategy to employ in this era. If they succeed in this attempt to turn government against government they will have achieved their goal of returning the world to the dark ages. The primary goal for all democracies that are the targets of terrorism should be to join forces against the terrorist organizations themselves. Preventive war against sovereign states suspected of harboring terrorists may occasionally be necessary, but Secretary-General Kofi Annan is certainly right to call for unity among the great powers in waging such wars.

It has been argued "Why worry?" The results of proliferation might not be so bad, even if nuclear weapons are developed and used, because the perpetrator can be destroyed by the overwhelming nuclear power of the United States. This argument was made by some who supported war in Iraq and who, at the same time, favored "living with" a nuclear-armed North Korea. They agreed that the spread of nuclear weapons is dangerous, but argued that the dangers, though real, could be managed. Scholars and analysts also have argued the general case that the United States can live comfortably with the spread of nuclear weapons, confident in the knowledge that rational leaders will understand the risks they face if they even think about unleashing nuclear war, and that this will make the world safer because regional rivals armed with nuclear weapons will be reluctant to go to war with each other.

Deterrence may indeed work in such circumstances, but new nuclear weapons in more hands increase the possibility that, at some point, deterrence will fail. As time goes by, the United States should not assume that its remoteness from unstable areas in Eurasia will save it from the millions of casualties that a single nuclear explosion could cause. The technology of long-distance delivery of nuclear weapons already is quite widespread, and U.S. borders are still porous. As we argue in this book, success in preventing the proliferation of nuclear weapons while building the future global security environment offers the best hope of avoiding the nuclear nightmares portrayed above.

II. Looking Forward

The Security Environment of the Future

If a cascade of events leading to the injection of nuclear weapons into regional conflicts around the world is anywhere near being a plausible scenario, what would the security environment look like?

- Greater availability of nuclear weapons for terrorists means that borders should be made entry-proof for any illicit cargo. But the war on drugs has shown this to be impossible. More intrusive police and intelligence activities would become necessary. The USA Patriot Act, and its implementation by the Bush administration's Justice Department, is a foretaste of things to come. The effects of this on civil liberties, and on the free flow of merchandise and travel by ordinary citizens, and, indeed, the effects on all normal aspects of life in the United States and elsewhere are incalculable, and potentially enormously harmful. Quite apart from the societal impact on democratic nations around the world, the economic effects are likely to be damaging, as the events following September 11, 2001, demonstrated.

- Nuclear crises in sensitive areas in the Middle East, South Asia, and East Asia will be more frequent, requiring both diplomacy and resort to military force to defuse. The Iraqi conflict and the India-Pakistan confrontation are examples of what can be expected.

- More calls will be heard for the U.S. military to respond to incipient nuclear programs through preventive or preemptive war, or to deploy forces to terminate local conflicts or to support a threatened friendly nation. Pressures will grow to withdraw from regions that could involve the United States in conflicts not seen as central to U.S. vital interests, even though this would not contribute to the long-run safety of the nation.

- Increased military budgets for several nations, and especially the United States, will be necessary as a result of pressures on governments to deal with nuclear crises.

- Advantages now accruing to the United States owing to its preponderance in conventional military power will be reduced. Nuclear weapons are the great equalizers. Their availability to many more nations will require a reassessment and probably a readjustment in U.S. doctrine regarding their use in limited conflicts.

- The consequences of an enhanced role for nuclear weapons in a role other than as weapons of last resort will include the strong possibility that these weapons will come to be regarded as quite usable as weapons of choice, including by the United States as it attacks deeply buried and hardened command posts and stockpiles of biological weapons.

- Nations previously dependent on the United States for the security provided by the U.S. "nuclear umbrella" will develop their own nuclear deterrent, thus dissolving one of the strongest ties between the United States and its current allies. Examples of this could include Germany, Japan, South Korea, Saudi Arabia, Taiwan, and Turkey. The result will be diminished influence for the United States and an effective end to the Non-Proliferation Treaty.

- The difficulty in managing nuclear crises in which more than two nuclear-armed states are involved, such as China, Taiwan, the United States, Japan, South or North Korea, will be much greater.

- There will be greater uncertainty about the sources of nuclear explosions, of knowing whether an accidental explosion was the beginning of a deliberate attack, and of knowing where an attacking weapon came from.

- The probability of nuclear accidents causing loss of life, environmental damage, and misinterpretations of the true causes of the events will be higher.

- Rivalries among friends or client states of the major powers, when these rivals are both armed with nuclear weapons, could, perhaps, lead to greater cooperation among the great powers to head off a conflict. But this is the less likely outcome. Much more likely is a repetition of what is already apparent in Iraq, Iran, and North Korea. The United States has been at odds with at least one, and generally more than one, of the major powers about applying economic pressure or threatening force in each one of these cases. This situation is the more probable indicator of what the future will be like. Nuclear weapons will be a potent wedge issue in relations among members of the UN Security Council.

Present-day concern about the impending demise of the non-proliferation regime and the spread of nuclear weapons is reflected in some of the voices in Washington which assume that U.S. military force, rather than patient diplomacy, is the way to resolve differences. The expectation that "the cult of the offensive" will be successful is reminiscent of the years preceding World War I. Most apparent is a disposition toward, and an ideological preference for, independent action at the expense of collective action, treaties, and international norms. Can such tendencies be altered? Is the world described above inevitable?

Motivations for Acquiring Nuclear Weapons

To answer both questions, it is necessary to look first at the motivations for national nuclear weapons programs. To block or roll back these programs, those motivations will have to be addressed, especially if diplomacy, rather than force, is to be the first instrument of choice. If policies or methods can be found that would respond to or alter those motivations, the bleak outlook described above may not be inevitable.

The cases of North Korea, Iran, and Iraq suggest that national security has been the basic driver of the decisions made by the governments of these countries in the nuclear arena. Parity with major opponents, prestige, and a quest for regional domination, or at least regional influence, have been part of the mix of incentives. Nor can more cynical motivations, such as extortion for financial aid by North Korea, be ruled out, though it is hard to deny that each of those nations has faced enemies, near or afar, who might pause before employing force against it and its regional interests if it possessed nuclear weapons. Saddam Hussein's decision to take Iraq into the rank of nuclear-armed states must have caused the Iranian government to decide that Iran also should have a nuclear deterrent—at some point.

Motivating each of these three countries, to a greater or lesser degree, almost certainly have been issues of sovereignty and national prestige, sometimes involving dreams of regional dominance. Here, the evidence is more speculative but there is little doubt that the leaders of each of these countries felt entitled to the same accouterments of power to which other nations are entitled. Indeed, a North Korean spokesperson said as much: the war in Iraq proves that the defense of national sovereignty requires a powerful deterrent, said the North Korean foreign ministry. Aside from the nuclear-armed Americans always looming over him, North Korea's leader, Kim Jong Il, probably sees his nuclear-armed, though currently friendly, neighbors, China and Russia, as potential adversaries and thinks his hand would be strengthened if North Korea also were a nuclear weapon state.

Iran sees Russia and the United States as nations with whom it would like to deal on a more equal footing, not to mention Israel. Furthermore, Iran's own self-image as a major regional power since antiquity probably feeds an interest in acquiring nuclear weapons.

Under Saddam Hussein, Iraq entertained visions of great power status, of being the predominant power in the Middle East. Quite apart from basic security considerations, those visions required Iraq to become a nuclear weapon state.

In each of these three cases, it is also likely that internal advocates of nuclear weapons have been influential with their governments, as also appears to have been the case in India and Pakistan. These internal advocates may be acting on behalf of a variety of parochial interests, ranging from professional pride to bureaucratic competition to budgetary considerations. It is probable that the military leaders in these three nations pressed for nuclear weapons, quite independently of what their leaders thought. And their arguments may well have resonated with these leaders not only for broad strategic reasons but also because of internal considerations. Leaders typically enhance their grip on power by providing strong programs and financial support to important constituencies within their bureaucracies.

The Practice of Preventive or Preemptive Military Action

Any anti-proliferation campaign, to be successful, must attack the sources of the problem. To focus only on nuclear weapons programs and to ignore the broader strategic and security context in which these programs have proceeded is a recipe for failure, as past experience demonstrates. And the use of the military instrument of U.S. foreign policy to deal with nuclear proliferation must be considered as part of an anti-proliferation campaign. The question, in this regard, is under what circumstances would it be advisable to use or threaten to use American military power in a preventive or preemptive mode. Preemptive action to prevent an impending military attack is a time-honored method of dealing with a clear-cut threat

of a certain type; there are questions of evidence and legitimacy, of course, but this is familiar ground for students
of international law. The more complex and controversial
issue is preventive war of the type that the United States
waged in Iraq and has suggested that it will wage elsewhere. For the purposes of this analysis, the question is
how critical will preventive or preemptive use of military
force be in stopping or rolling back nuclear aspirations.
Are these methods an essential and central part of an anti-
proliferation campaign, or an important, but sparingly
used tool? Could a preventive war doctrine be an incitement, in some cases, to nuclear proliferation?

In his joint press conference with Prime Minister Tony
Blair on January 31, 2003, President Bush said:

> The strategic view of America changed after September
> 11th. We must deal with threats before they hurt the
> American people again. . . . After September the 11th,
> the doctrine of containment just doesn't hold any water,
> as far as I'm concerned. . . . My vision shifted dramati-
> cally after September the 11th, because I now realize
> the stakes.

In its "National Security Strategy of the United States
of America" (September 17, 2002), President Bush's
national security team also wrote about "taking anticipa-
tory action to defend ourselves, even if uncertainty
remains as to the time and place of the enemy's attack,"
and about acting against emerging threats "before they
are fully formed." President Bush has declared that if
weapons of mass destruction are part of the equation,
preemption could come too late to save the United States
from massive harm. Therefore, he is driven to a policy of

preventive wars—that is, a policy that requires the United States to take military action, or threaten such action, to blunt or eliminate a military threat involving weapons of mass destruction that might not emerge until years in the future. Much has been written about the implications— ethical, juridical, and political—if such a policy were to be systematically pursued. In this book, the precedents and potential application of such a policy will be examined.

Until the 2003 Iraq war, the best-known examples of military force being used to block or delay the development of nuclear weapons, either deliberately or inadvertently, were the Israeli attack on Iraq's Osirak reactor in 1981 and the U.S.-led coalition's attack on Iraq in 1991. The carefully calculated Israeli strike did not diminish Saddam Hussein's determination to build an Iraqi nuclear weapon, but it bought a few years' time—a not inconsequential outcome, although not a lasting solution.

The use of force by the United States and its coalition partners during the Persian Gulf war of 1991 was a response to Saddam Hussein's invasion of Kuwait, but it had the inadvertent effect of destroying Iraq's effort to acquire nuclear weapons. At the time, Iraq was perhaps within two or three years of achieving an initial bomb by a different, and unanticipated, technology of electromagnetic isotope separation to enrich uranium for bomb fuel. Subsequently, under UN supervision, Hussein's nuclear infrastructure was dismantled to the point where, in 2003, the International Atomic Energy Agency (IAEA) was unable to discover that any of it remained effective for producing nuclear weapons. At this writing, many weeks after the war ended, that remains the case.

Another well-known case where the U.S. government

came close to using force was during the North Korean nuclear crisis of 1993–94. North Korea had made overt moves toward using plutonium derived from an alleged civilian nuclear power program to fabricate nuclear weapons. It had defied pressure applied by the United States and other nations and had announced its withdrawal from the nuclear Non-Proliferation Treaty. The Clinton administration threatened to impose sanctions, which North Korea said would be an act of war. Faced with this situation, the U.S. Defense Department, according to public reports, made plans to destroy the North Korean nuclear facilities. This would have been a preventive attack had it been made, but it never was, instead becoming an example of coercive diplomacy. Seemingly at the last moment, former president Carter opened a door to a deal with the North Korean president at the time, the late Kim Il Sung. That resulted, in 1994, in an Agreed Framework designed to freeze and then roll back the North Korean nuclear weapons program. The episode is an example of using a threat of force to delay, but not terminate, a nuclear weapons program.

Other examples of nuclear rollback have been accomplished without the use or threat of force, but with diplomatic pressure, and, sometimes, economic help. These cases include Ukraine, Kazakhstan, Belarus, Argentina, and Brazil. South Africa ended its program as the era of apartheid rule was ending. South Korea, which reportedly had an incipient nuclear weapons program in the late 1970s, ended it when threatened with the withdrawal of American military guarantees of that country's security. Nonetheless, military force, or the threat of force, was successful in three cases—Iraq in 1981 and, inadvertently,

1991; North Korea in 1993–94—in delaying the acquisition of nuclear weapons by potential proliferants. The Cuban missile crisis of 1962 also was a textbook example of the marriage of the threat of force and diplomacy to head off a potential nuclear threat, but it involved the deployment, not the acquisition, of nuclear weapons.

Assessing the Utility of Preventive or Preemptive Military Action

Can the success of using or threatening to use force in three instances—four, if the 2003 Iraq war is included—be taken as models for what should be done to delay, block, or roll back nuclear proliferation? The relevant lessons to be learned from these instances are as follows:

- Military force, or the threat of it, was usable when the likelihood of successful retaliation against the homelands of the attacking powers by the potential proliferant was low (Iraq in 1981 and 2003; North Korea in 1993).

- Military force was usable or potentially usable when the proliferant was viewed by large parts of the international community as a threat to its neighbors (North Korea in 1993; arguably Iraq in 2003).

- Military force became an option when peaceful means of blocking nuclear weapons programs had failed or seemed unlikely to work (Iraq in 1981, and, arguably, 2003; North Korea in 1993).

Those three conditions almost certainly will all have to exist in a particular case if a proposed use of military force is to gain the broadest possible support, not only for the military action itself but also for the follow-through, economic and otherwise. To support this judgment, there are several other cases where not all three conditions existed, and, in particular, military force or the threat of force was not usable or particularly credible, and it was not brought into play. They include the Soviet Union in the 1950s as it tested and began to deploy nuclear weapons, and China, when it began to move toward a nuclear weapons capability in the 1960s.

There were voices, even influential voices, in the United States that spoke out for preventive war against the Soviet Union in the 1950s, fearing that a Soviet nuclear arsenal would prove devastating for America's position in the world and for the American homeland itself. Neither President Truman, who was not entirely convinced that this particular Soviet threat existed, nor President Eisenhower, who knew that it did but believed it could be deterred, gave any serious thought to preventive war. Eisenhower's philosophy was that the United States and the Soviet Union were in for a long-term struggle and that containment was the only answer. He was deeply troubled, not only about the effects of a nuclear war, which he regarded as horrendous, but also about the long-term problems of dealing with a Soviet Union that had become a wasteland. He thought about the follow-through. And so, to that American leader, the use or threat of force to block Soviet acquisition of nuclear weapons was not an option.

Of course Eisenhower presumed that nuclear weapons would be used in the case of a general war with the Soviet Union. Some current administration strategists appear to believe that the threats now visible might be handled through conventional-only preventive war, an easier task for the decision maker. The closer the targeted state is to acquiring weapons of mass destruction, however, the less certain that premise will be.

A similar discussion took place at high levels of the American and Soviet governments during the Kennedy administration when China was seen to be nearing a nuclear weapons capability. The discussion led nowhere, another example of the disutility of military force under the circumstances then existing.

In other cases the use of force was not necessary, and was very unlikely even to be considered. These include South Africa, Argentina, Brazil, Kazakhstan, Belarus, and Ukraine. North Korea in 2002–2003 may also be a highly relevant case although it is too early to say. The South African nuclear program was not generally known to exist, but it lasted only a few years before being dismantled. Argentina and Brazil accommodated themselves to a non-nuclear status for political and diplomatic reasons. Ukraine, Belarus, and Kazakhstan gave in to U.S. and Russian political pressure and economic blandishments. Ukraine also received a form of security assurance from the United States.

These situations may also be taken as illustrations of a generic situation: where determination to build and to keep nuclear weapons on the part of potential proliferants is not very strong, military force is not needed in the policy equation. One could also ask whether the use of U.S. military force against such countries would ever have been considered. The answer is unknown, but it seems in retrospect to have been very unlikely.

Having discussed situations where force might be used, the opposite question should be addressed: in which generic situations is force unlikely to be used to block nuclear proliferation?

- Military force is not likely to be used when the costs of doing so are judged to be higher than allowing proliferation to occur (Soviet Union, 1950s; China, 1960s).

- Military force is not likely to be used when the proliferant government is perceived as being legitimate and sufficiently responsible so as to be deterrable (again, the Soviet Union and China).

- Military force, or even the threat of force, will not be used if diplomatic efforts could plausibly succeed in blocking or rolling back proliferation (South Africa, Argentina, Brazil, Belarus, Ukraine, Kazakhstan; North Korea after the 1994 U.S.–North Korean Agreed Framework).

- Military force or the threat of such force is not likely to be used in the cases of friendly or democratically inclined countries (Israel and India, for example). A close reading of Bush administration statements suggests that, in such cases, strong diplomatic pressure would not be used either.

The conclusion from this analysis is that military force or the threat of using such force is quite circumscribed in its application to the problem of nuclear proliferation. In most of the future cases that can be imagined, force in a preventive war sense would not be considered.

So where would U.S. military force be considered in the future? The list is short. It is limited to states widely considered to be run by tyrants with a history of threatening aggressive tendencies and to sub-state groups that appear to have embarked on the course of acquiring nuclear weapons but have not yet done so. Iraq was the prime example of the first category. It is clear that factors apart from worries about nuclear proliferation and links to terrorism were in play that strongly reinforced the determination of the Bush administration to wage war against Iraq. President Bush cited these in his speech of February 26, 2003. They included: "Example of freedom for other nations in the region"; "A new stage for Middle Eastern peace"; "A clear warning that support for terror will not be tolerated"; "No excuse to leave the Iraqi regime's torture chambers and poison labs in operation." The experience of the 2003 Iraq war suggests that for the American people, at least, an emerging new principle of international law carries great weight: brutal treatment inflicted by a government on its own people can be considered a threat to international peace and security justifying military intervention. Postwar public opinion in the United States deems the Iraq war to have been justified on human rights grounds, even though weapons of mass destruction were not found, at this writing.

There are not many other countries that fit all the criteria. Libya comes to mind, and possibly Cuba and Syria would fit the profile, but none of these countries is quite "roguish" enough and none has a serious nuclear weapons program. They could become the hosts for international terrorist groups, which might trigger an attack. The most notorious cases of potential proliferants, of course, are North Korea and Iran. North Korea has a credible deterrent in its conventional military forces. When U.S. troops are withdrawn from forward positions in South Korea, the Pentagon might then be freer to launch a preventive attack on North Korea, but with both South Korea and Japan in the position of being hostages, and likely to suffer immense damage if North Korea chose to respond, a powerful deterrent to U.S. offensive action would continue to exist. Iran has a nascent democratic movement and more international support than Saddam Hussein ever enjoyed. Conditions may exist in the future in Iran that could meet the criteria for military intervention, but they do not exist now.

There are two other generic situations that must be considered to round out an analysis of the circumstances under which U.S. military force might be used. The first is a situation where a nation close to the realization of a nuclear weapons capability shows unmistakable signs of an intention to attack another nation. Those signs could range from public or private statements to preparations to launch a ballistic missile. A U.S. attack in this situation would be preemption, however, not a case of preventive war.

The second situation is one in which other major nations—all other nuclear weapon states, for example—have jointly agreed with the United States that a particular nation's acquisition of nuclear weapons would be a threat to international peace and security. In this case, an attack could be preventive or preemptive depending on how imminent the threat.

These two situations bring the discussion into the realm of legitimacy, as customarily defined by the international community. International law, including the UN Charter, accepts the principle that defense against aggression is lawful and morally justified, quite apart from the question of whether nuclear weapons are a part of the picture. Preemption has been an accepted principle of international law for a very long time. Preventive war does not enjoy that status, although it has often figured in balance of power calculations throughout history. The UN Charter (Chapter VII), also explicitly permits the use of force when necessary to restore international peace and security when authorized by the Security Council, even when members of the Security Council are not themselves the victims of aggression.

There are other actions available to the United States in cases where military force is not the right answer. In fact, a main theme of this book is that diplomacy, backed by all the instruments of national power, is generally going to be the right response to the threat of nuclear proliferation. "Regime change," for example, can be the best solution to the problem, as the Bush administration argued in the case of Iraq. But this can be attained through internal processes that do not require the use or threat of use of American military power. "Societal change," in fact, is a better way of describing these processes. The United States cannot dictate such changes but it can encourage and support them. This will be discussed in connection with individual case studies at the end of this book.

The Terrorist Threat

The danger that terrorists or non-state actors will acquire a usable nuclear weapons capability should be neither exaggerated nor minimized. The most direct way for them to achieve such a capability would be through theft, or illegal purchase. Aside from especially designed devices such as the notorious "suitcase bomb" referred to by the late General Lebed of Russia, nuclear devices are not small, though they are readily mobile. Depending upon their level of sophistication or contemplated deployment options, many devices have some sort of permissive action link, or control mechanisms designed to prevent unauthorized detonation. These may include disarming mechanisms that will disable the weapon upon receipt of incorrect signals.

The most important means for minimizing the risk of terrorists' acquiring a nuclear weapon is the extension and aggressive application of cooperative threat reduction measures, first developed in the 1990s under the Nunn-Lugar legislation for the former Soviet Union. Technology is available, and should be supported, for effective material protection, control, and accountability. An example of a security measure that merits receiving more attention would be the installation of radiation detectors at transit points at national borders. At present, many of the exit and entrance points on the borders of the former Soviet Union are not so equipped.

As to whether a terrorist or non-state organization could actually develop or create its own nuclear weapon, the most difficult step is to acquire the fuel for a nuclear explosion, that is, plutonium or highly enriched uranium. A substantial economic and technical investment is required to build and operate a facility for indigenous production of such special nuclear materials. To do so covertly is very challenging and is unlikely to succeed. Once in possession of the necessary quantity of special nuclear materials, the path to a workable bomb, even of the simplest type—a gun-type uranium bomb like the untested one that the United States dropped over Hiroshima on August 6, 1945—is still far from easy. It is more challenging to build a plutonium bomb that requires, for detonation, a carefully designed and time-coordinated implosion mechanism to initiate a fission chain reaction. But for a primitive single-stage fission device the technical information is widely available, and it is too late to do much about preventing its further dissemination. The best means for denial of a nuclear capability to terrorists or sub-state organizations is to provide maximum protection for existing stockpiles of weapons and nuclear materials that can be used as fuel for nuclear weapons, and, additionally to reduce the size of the weapons stockpiles and begin to modify the existing nuclear materials to make them no longer readily usable as fuel for weapons. A universal treaty that would cap the production of fissile material for weapons purposes, long under discussion in the Conference on Disarmament in Geneva, would also be useful.

The relative ease of acquiring or producing biological pathogens or chemical agents that are far less costly, and do not require a major infrastructure and development program, suggests that this is a more likely path for acquiring weapons intended to cause mass terror. There is also the possibility of building radiological dispersal devices, the so-called "dirty bombs." They are basically high explosives mixed with relatively long-lived (months to years) radioactive isotopes, such as cesium 137, strontium 90, or cobalt 60. In today's era of suicidal terrorism there would be no need to shield the individuals delivering such a weapon from being incapacitated by radiation, since the cumulative dose would hardly affect or incapacitate them during the minutes or hours of accomplishing a delivery.

The focus in this book has been limited to the nuclear weapons danger, and what can and should be done to reduce it. But it is evident from this discussion that cooperative threat reduction programs such as Nunn-Lugar are of vital importance to prevent the spread of other weapons capable of mass terror—biological, chemical, and radiological.

A particularly pressing issue at this time is whether it is possible to agree on actionable criteria against terrorist or sub-state entities that are developing or attempting to develop nuclear capabilities, or against the states that are harboring them. This is a new challenge for the world community.

The experience at the United Nations leading up to the invasion of Iraq shows how difficult that challenge will be. If there is a need to restore the international consensus that nuclear proliferation should be prevented, it must begin with building a consensus within the UN Security Council on what to do about terrorists and their access to nuclear weapons. Restoring and increasing confidence in the IAEA as a nuclear monitoring agency also will be necessary in the aftermath of its efforts to inspect Iraq, efforts that were terminated while still in progress, and prematurely so in the eyes of many. The return of IAEA personnel to Iraq for a meaningful role in investigating Iraq's nuclear infrastructure would be a beneficial first step.

More than a decade ago, in January 1992, the UN Security Council discussed the spreading capacity of nations around the globe to produce or otherwise acquire weapons of mass destruction. The Council concluded that this represented a threat to international peace and security.

On September 21, 1992, President George H. W. Bush proposed, in a speech at the United Nations, that "the

Security Council should become a key forum for non-pro-liferation enforcement." The Security Council's 16–0 vote in support of a resolution requiring Iraq's nuclear (and biological and chemical) disarmament in November 2002, showed that a consensus exists favoring anti-proliferation policies. Despite the Council's inability to achieve a consensus concerning military action against Iraq in March 2003, the first President Bush's idea has merit and a strong effort should be made to implement that proposal. Among the ideas that his administration floated in 1992 was that a cell should be established at United Nations headquarters to advise the Security Council on nuclear proliferation problems. That was never acted upon, except in the form of the United Nations Special Commission (UNSCOM) established in 1991 and the United Nations Monitoring, Verification, and Inspections Commission (UNMOVIC), established in 1999 for biological and chemical weapons, both concerned with Iraq. The IAEA was pressed into service to deal with the special case of Iraq's nuclear potential.

The United Nations Secretariat has been strengthened significantly since 1992 in its ability to assist the Security Council with peacekeeping issues. UNMOVIC also has a strong staff in the area of biological and chemical weapons. Nothing on the required scale has been done at UN Headquarters with regard to the deadly threat of nuclear terrorism and proliferation. An important step in restoring the unity and effectiveness of the Security Council would be to adopt a resolution requesting the UN secretary-general, in close coordination with the IAEA, to strengthen the IAEA's presence in New York to help the Security Council deal with these matters.

Furthermore, the IAEA, as part of a move to strengthen

its enforcement mechanism, should be directed to propose to the Security Council a plan for linking the suppression of nuclear terrorism to the Chapter VII peace-enforcement authority that the UN Charter confers upon the Security Council.

A prime purpose of such an anti-terrorism operation would be to establish plausible links between a terrorist organization and an identified supplier source of nuclear materials or nuclear weapons-related equipment. An authorization, in that case, might be given to nations concerned to interdict shipments by sea or air of fissile material and, perhaps, the means of their delivery. As the Bush administration's Proliferation Security Initiative (PSI) in this area suggests, unilateral military action might be required because of lack of time to act. But if possible, it would be desirable to conduct interdiction operations under a general UN Security Council authorization. An example might be a decision to impose a Cuba-style quarantine around North Korea. In such a case, support by Japan, China, and Russia would be critically important, and an advance blessing by the UN would be helpful.

Is it wise to embroil the United Nations and the IAEA in such controversial matters so soon after the highly divisive debate over Iraq? The sooner the rebuilding process begins, the sooner the wounds will heal. An indication that the United States still has faith in the United Nations would encourage other nations to cooperate in enhancing its capability. And dealing with nuclear weapons in the context of what President G. W. Bush has called "the crossroads of radicalism and technology" should attract the support of nations that are genuinely worried about global terrorism. The first President Bush had it right in his proposal of September 21, 1992.

III. Denial Policies

Denial Policies at the Level of States

The likelihood that U.S. military force will have a rather limited role in forestalling nuclear proliferation means that most of the weight of the anti-proliferation effort will have to be carried by diplomacy with the essential backing of credible military strength. The United States has relied heavily on policies designed to prevent or inhibit potential proliferants from acquiring the necessary technology, weapons-usable materials, and equipment, including dual-use equipment. U.S. diplomacy has also been devoted to creating international organizations and rules to support a denial policy. Those organizations and rules are not only still needed but should be strengthened. Loosening restrictions on transfer of engineering information, nuclear materials, or equipment, beyond those transfers mandated under a rigorous inspection regime for signatory nations under Article IV of the NPT, would weaken the norms that discourage proliferation, as well as accelerate the spread of nuclear weapons capabilities. These restrictions are especially critical in blocking access by terrorist groups to nuclear materials, but they must be supplemented by the use of force, when required, and supported by economic measures that encourage compliance by governments and industries.

The challenge to prevent nations, as opposed to terrorist or sub-state organizations, from acquiring nuclear weapons has become very difficult. Nations might have access to uranium deposits in their territory and to the assets and technical base to produce weapons indigenously. Efforts already have been made by some countries to import specialized components for a centrifuge system that would be capable of producing enough highly enriched uranium to develop a few bombs over a multimonth period. This is a significant undertaking, and to keep track of it requires good intelligence on construction activity together with cooperative information sources on commercial activity. The same applies to other possible uranium-enrichment technologies. Underground production facilities present a verification challenge, for which a combination of surveillance by technical means and signal intercepts, together with human sources, would have to be employed. Recent experience with the uranium program initiated by North Korea shows the importance of gaining information on efforts to import the needed technology. The bottom line in this case is this: one cannot count on a lack of technical information preventing would-be proliferators from developing nuclear weapons. Denying proliferators access to special nuclear materials is the best line of defense.

Greater care also needs to be taken with export controls. Under the Non-Proliferation Treaty, nuclear weapon states were encouraged to provide the non-nuclear states assistance that they needed to reap the peaceful benefits and uses of nuclear energy. That was the basic deal that caused non–nuclear weapon states to accept the limitations of the treaty. The sovereign rights of buyers or sellers of exports relevant to nuclear facilities were limited by an understanding among supplier countries that, in effect, prohibited the transfer of technology specifically applicable for fabricating a nuclear weapon. But dual-use technology always presented a difficult problem.

It is now up to the nuclear suppliers to agree to and police even stronger restrictions on the sale or transfer of items that could be used for weapons production by non-nuclear countries. For example, gas centrifuges have become a very important part of the nuclear programs of Iran and North Korea, and were alleged to be important in the U.S. National Intelligence Estimate (October 2002) in Saddam Hussein's program prior to the Gulf war in 1991. Any component that could be useful in building these uranium-enrichment machines is capable of contributing to nuclear proliferation and is closely monitored by intelligence agencies. Governments must do a better job than they have of controlling the export of this and other equipment applicable for developing nuclear weapons. Unless these types of transactions can be stopped, the whole non-proliferation effort will be seriously undermined. There is a downside in facing this problem, which is that restrictions on sales of equipment that could be useful for building nuclear weapons can be applied too broadly and, in the process, cause harm by inhibiting useful scientific cooperation. The answer lies in complete transparency concerning transfers of even remotely sensitive equipment, and the scientific community should insist on this.

Denial policies can, at best, only slow down nuclear weapons proliferation. The technology of manufacturing nuclear weapons is widely available throughout the world. Second- and third-tier nations can be sources of equipment. The deal struck by Pakistan and North Korea is an excellent example of this: Pakistan reportedly provided assistance to North Korea in building a gas centrifuge plant to enrich uranium, and, in exchange, North Korea provided ballistic missile assistance to Pakistan. Soon, if things go badly, there may be as many nuclear weapon states outside as inside the NPT regime. It is still not so easy for some countries to acquire uranium ore, but that, too, is not an insuperable obstacle for nations determined to acquire it, and several non–nuclear weapon states have uranium located within their territories.

The Problem of Monitoring
Nuclear Proliferation Activities

In today's world the monitoring of nuclear proliferation and nuclear weapons–related activities is extremely demanding. The evidence for this has become clear over the past decade from the activities and disclosures about the programs in Iraq and North Korea. That experience also emphasizes the importance of being able to detect efforts to acquire nuclear weapons at early stages. This presents a challenge to intelligence efforts as a whole rather than to technical intelligence alone. Intelligence acquired by national technical means plays an important supporting role but it alone cannot do the job without an effective human intelligence capability and on-site challenge inspection authority.

The model of monitoring nuclear activities of the Soviet Union during the Cold War is not appropriate for the task of detecting efforts by proliferants who want to acquire nuclear technology. In the case of the Soviet Union the nuclear problem was defined in terms of finding and monitoring large plutonium production facilities, and detecting the deployment of large nuclear forces, a relatively straightforward task for U.S. "national technical means"— that is, satellites viewing the earth from orbits circling several hundred kilometers above it. With their broad repertoire of electro-optical, infrared, and radar sensors they can track the construction of new large facilities, the levels of activity at known facilities, and also the deployment levels of strategic nuclear forces. The task now is to detect relatively small nuclear production activities in a number of countries that are potential proliferators. However, to go beyond indications that arouse suspicions and in fact confirm that serious covert efforts toward a nuclear capability are being attempted, authority to make on-site challenge inspections will be very valuable, if not necessary.

It is clear that the intelligence problems facing the United States today are more demanding than those during the Cold War. U.S. intelligence agencies, working together with other nations' agencies as appropriate, must now worry not just about one superpower and its large and readily located nuclear installations. They also have to gather actionable intelligence on plans, intentions, and programs by organizations in many geographical areas that could pose serious threats to the U.S. homeland, to other states, and to U.S. interests abroad. Increasingly, governments and terrorist groups are acquiring technologies, home-grown as well as imported, that can be readily hidden, require only modest investment, and pose dangerous threats. There is no question that good intelligence, starting with good human intelligence, good analysis, and reliance on the best science and technology available, is a key component to U.S. security. "Exquisite" intelligence, in the words of the Bush administration's 2002 Nuclear Posture Review, on any adversaries' plans and intentions, as well as their capabilities, is indeed an important goal. This emphasizes the point that just collecting information is not enough. The full value added comes in being able to interpret information about what other governments and terrorist groups are doing, applying first-rate technical expertise, based on openly available as well as on covert information. Good information is a sine qua non, but interpretation and understanding are increasingly becoming the coin of the realm for intelligence. To achieve it will require highly capable and trained people knowledgeable in the languages and habits of many diverse cultures. This must be a priority commitment of the U.S. intelligence community.

The intelligence challenge to discover that a nation has initiated a serious effort to build a nuclear weapon is illustrated by the following example. Assume the would-be proliferator has access to adequate uranium deposits in its territory, as well as the technical base and assets to produce nuclear weapons indigenously. A particular technology of concern for proliferators seeking to acquire nuclear weapons is the gas centrifuge to produce highly enriched uranium (HEU). As already noted, several nations have made serious efforts to import specialized components for centrifuge systems that might be capable of producing enough highly enriched uranium to develop a few bombs over a multi-month period. To get a rough idea of the size of such an enterprise consider the requirements to build a gun-type fission bomb relying on the simplest technology. Such a weapon can be developed and deployed without nuclear explosive testing. It is fueled by HEU, which is produced by separating the isotope U^{235} from natural uranium, 100 kilograms of which contain just 0.7 kilograms of U^{235}. The standard measure of energy for enriching the U^{235} content of a sample of natural uranium with gas centrifuge systems is the separative work unit, or SWU. In order to enrich a sufficient quantity of natural uranium to provide the fuel for one gun-type uranium bomb requires roughly 14,000 SWUs. With currently available technology each gas centrifuge is capable of about 4 SWUs each year. To produce just one primitive HEU weapon in a year would therefore require perhaps 3,500 centrifuge machines, depending on their efficiency.

Such technology for gas centrifuge machines is the result of many years of effort and billions of dollars of investment. Special materials are needed for the very rapidly spinning centrifuge columns. This means that a substantial investment must be made in the capital plant, but the overall energy requirements are low compared with other technologies for enriching natural uranium to bomb fuel. More advanced versions of gas centrifuge machines are now able to operate at a level of up to, perhaps, 40 SWUs per year per machine. With this newer technology no more than 350 machines could provide fuel for one primitive HEU bomb per year. The large halls at the uranium enrichment facility recently observed at Natanz in Iran are estimated, by David Albright and Carey Hinderstein of the Institute for Science and International Security, to be capable of holding over 50,000 centrifuges that would have a capacity to fuel a dozen or more uranium bombs per year.

In spite of all that is now known and is widely available

in the public domain about nuclear technology, building up a functioning nuclear weapons program is not a trivial task. It still requires substantial efforts involving large numbers of trained people, particularly with specialized engineering and scientific skills, in dealing, for example, with maraging steel needed for high-speed centrifuges, as well as steady multiyear funding to build and operate such a plant. Nevertheless, if a proliferating country wished to conceal a gas centrifuge plant capable of enriching uranium to fuel several weapons per year, the required facility could be contained on a factory floor space of modest size. It would require less than a megawatt of electric power input and could be readily hidden underground. This emphasizes the importance of monitoring from the very beginning of the construction, together with insisting on authority for on-site challenge inspections once a suspicious activity has been identified. This will almost certainly require on-site inspection measures as provided for in the Additional Protocol that the IAEA is trying to negotiate with its member states. But stronger enforcement measures will be required to back up the Protocol. It is a good step forward, but as suggested elsewhere in this book, it does not deal with the case where a nation refuses to admit or give access to inspectors nor are there any clear downsides to simply refusing to accept the Protocol.

If a country with the technology at the level of North Korea or Iraq were to choose to go the more difficult route of producing weapons grade plutonium for an implosion weapon, it would have to construct a power reactor and plutonium separation plant. These would be difficult to construct covertly. Furthermore, in order to extract plutonium by reprocessing of their radiated reactor fuel, the proliferator would have to conceal any evidence indicative of reprocessing, for example, the radioactive isotope krypton 85, which is an unambiguous signature of this process. However, to be useful as an indicator of such an activity, the signal of krypton 85 must be obtained by air samples very close to a suspect facility since it must exceed the background signal from the global atmospheric burden of krypton 85.

These observations give a picture of the scale of effort and difficulty involved in detecting and/or hiding nuclear production activities.

The Role of Ballistic Missile Defense

The current administration has emphasized the need for deploying a missile defense system to protect the U.S. homeland from the threat of limited attacks by nuclear-armed ballistic missiles that may be launched by a hostile proliferant power. This led the United States to take a long-debated, controversial decision to withdraw from the 1972 Anti-Ballistic Missile (ABM) Treaty.

The rationale stated in the Bush administration's 2002 "Nuclear Posture Review" was that

> the demonstration of a range of technologies and systems for missile defense can have a dissuasive effect on potential adversaries. The problem of countering missile defenses, especially defensive systems with multiple layers, presents a potential adversary with the prospect of a difficult, time-consuming and expensive undertaking.

The thrust of this statement is that the administration

views ballistic missile defenses as one element, and an important one, of an anti-proliferation policy.

Prior to President Bush's decision to withdraw from the ABM Treaty effective in 2002, in order to move ahead with plans for a limited national missile defense, it had been recognized that some of the restrictions of the Treaty had become dated in the post–Cold War world. These included restrictions that severely limited testing of new concepts and possibilities for such a system. During the dangerous years of U.S.-Soviet confrontation, those restrictions were believed to be appropriate on technical as well as strategic grounds in terms of their stabilizing value. Although good reasons remain to be skeptical of the ultimate potential of ballistic missile defenses against advanced ballistic missile threats, in view of technical limitations, there are now valid reasons to study and learn what might feasibly be done to protect the United States and allies against more primitive threats, or from entities against which deterrence alone may be inadequate.

The capabilities of ballistic missile defenses utilizing current or foreseeable technologies against long-range ballistic missile threats that employ countermeasures are very limited. How effective such technologies will prove to be in dissuading adversaries like North Korea and Iran from developing and deploying long-range ballistic missiles armed with nuclear, or biological and chemical, warheads, remains to be seen. At the moment there is no evidence that the U.S. ballistic missile defense program is having an impact on North Korea's program to develop nuclear weapons. There is no doubt, however, about the impact of a North Korean nuclear weapons arsenal on a friendly state like Japan. A Japanese nuclear weapons program would ultimately be the response. Preventing such an outcome is a most important goal for U.S. anti-proliferation policy; this would signal a breakdown of the non-proliferation regime.

Whatever level of success may actually be achieved by a limited ballistic missile defense against a relatively primitive attack, there are other means for delivering nuclear destruction against which such a defense is useless. These means include transport by sea aboard commercial ships or aboard large cargo vessels within a standard shipping container, perhaps hidden in the large worldwide drug traffic. Relatively short-range cruise missiles, or more primitive drones launched from the decks of commercial ships, are also a possibility as are commercial aircraft. None of these threat options is a sure thing for a world at alert status, but they cannot be dismissed as not credible.

A fact sheet on "National Policy on Ballistic Missile Defense" issued by the White House on May 20, 2003, proposes a broader international role for missile defense:

> Because the threats of the 21st century also endanger our friends and allies around the world, it is essential that we work together to defend against these threats. Missile defense cooperation will be a feature of U.S. relations with close, long-standing allies, and an important means to build new relationships with new friends like Russia.

Success in building cooperation in ballistic missile defense could encourage cooperation among nations in their common effort to extend and strengthen the nuclear non-proliferation regime. This argues in favor of U.S. efforts to seek broad international cooperation rather than proceeding unilaterally in deploying such systems. Moreover, a program to deploy weapons in space as part of a missile defense system would be challenging a broad international consensus against putting weapons in space. Such a development is one of the possibilities discussed in the White House fact sheet on ballistic missile defense, which calls for development of space-based interceptors for boost-phase and mid-course missile defense systems. This proposal raises the issue of whether such a development would be in the U.S. interest, given this country's heavy reliance on space-based sensors for intelligence as well as for navigational purposes. The importance of retaining the current condition of space as a (relatively) safe harbor for U.S. satellite systems should be weighed very carefully before the United States adds space as a new dimension for military competition. The lure of space dominance may seem attractive today in view of U.S. technical prowess, but history has shown that such technical edges cannot be relied on for long.

IV. Defining Diplomacy's Task

IF NEITHER THE military instrument, nor denial policies, nor ballistic missile defenses are likely to be completely effective in blocking or rolling back nuclear weapons proliferation, other diplomatic tools will have to carry a heavy load, appropriately backed up by military force. Before examining how other diplomatic tools could be sharpened and deployed in new ways, the strategic task these tools should seek to accomplish must be defined.

In the nightmare world depicted earlier in this book, nuclear weapons proliferation accelerated, owing to a complete breakdown of the restraints that were effectively used during most of the last half century. It is certainly possible to do better than that—but only if the patient practice of diplomacy is employed, in view of the limited utility of direct military means and of denial policies. The consequences of the nightmare world are so grave that the United States and its friends must dedicate themselves to preventing it.

There are two general outcomes that the United States should consider. They are as follows:

- *Rollback.* Nascent nuclear weapons capabilities, as in North Korea and Iran, should be dismantled. Nuclear weapons programs of other nations that are undeclared or de facto nuclear weapon states should be scaled back and ultimately dismantled. This would also be the ultimate, if distant, goal for all declared nuclear weapon states with no exception, as required by the Non-Proliferation Treaty.

- *Hold the line.* The present declared, undeclared, or de facto nuclear weapon states (United States, Russia, China, United Kingdom, France, Israel, India, Pakistan) would be the only nations to be included in that category. All other national nuclear weapons programs would be blocked and dismantled. The eight nuclear weapon states would make every effort to prevent nuclear arms competitions among themselves.

There is a third outcome, gradual proliferation, which some analysts think of as inevitable, and maybe even desirable in some cases. The issue of gradual proliferation has not been raised by the Bush administration as one of its concerns as regards friendly states. But this outcome should be described in terms of a policy goal so that its full implications can be discerned:

- *Gradual proliferation.* The goal would be to slow down nuclear weapons proliferation rather than to block it all together. The means utilized would generally be the traditional ones of denial, alliances, and global norms. The purpose, referring to the writings of Kenneth Waltz, would be to give the international system time to absorb new power relationships, including possible beneficial changes in leadership, and to adjust to them. It would be understood that exceptions to this policy might include the elimination of nuclear weapons programs in the hands of leaders known for their aggressive tendencies. In addition, the United States could provide to certain friends or allies the necessary nuclear means to balance a nuclear-armed rival (for example, help South Korea with a two-key nuclear system if North Korea becomes a de facto nuclear weapon state).

Rollback policies should be the preferred option for the United States from a narrowly self-interested point of view. The U.S. military advantage in modern, advanced-technology weapons would be heightened if nuclear weapons were less salient or, preferably, diminished substantially as a factor in interstate military relations. From a more disinterested, global standpoint, nuclear weapons present a serious threat to the safety and well-being of humanity and human civilization.

Holding the line at eight states would be a minimally acceptable outcome for the United States for the foreseeable future. This conclusion is based on the same logic that caused Article VI to be written into the nuclear Non-Proliferation Treaty. It is impossible for non–nuclear weapon states to accept that their sovereignties will be forever limited while those of a privileged few will not be. Anti-proliferation policies that are selective in excluding all current nuclear states cannot, in the long term, be successful. In today's world, as can be seen from almost daily events, simply holding the line has not contributed to a global anti-proliferation environment. And to many it is an incentive to proliferation.

The Bush administration's "National Strategy to Combat Weapons of Mass Destruction" (December 2002) declared that for some states "these are not weapons of last resort, but militarily useful weapons of choice." That is evidently true and so it is very much in the U.S. interest to make such nations pariahs by delegitimizing nuclear weapons as weapons of choice. To accomplish this, it should be U.S. policy that the purpose of such weapons so long as they exist, which will be for a very long time, should be solely to deter the use of nuclear weapons by other nations that continue to hold them, or to retaliate against states that use them, if it comes to that. U.S. policy should seek, through all means available, to make nuclear weapons less usable—for example, less reliance on prompt launch procedures, deactivation, separate storage of warheads, cooperation in early warning, reductions in holdings, and an obvious and unmistakable intention on the part of the United States to limit its reliance on nuclear weapons to absolutely last-resort conditions.

A gradual increase in nuclear weapon states, although better than the alternative of accelerated proliferation, will increase the hazards of deliberate or accidental nuclear weapons use. In this era, it will increase the chance of a terrorist-delivered nuclear weapon being detonated in an American city. The United States should declare its opposition to such an outcome, which would inevitably contribute to legitimizing nuclear weapons. They would come to be seen as an acceptable and necessary part of any serious nation's arsenal of weapons. And it should be understood that, although political relations can change and enemies can become friends, nuclear weapons are a permanent threat to humanity, no matter where they reside.

The Power of U.S. Example

There is a fallacy often heard in debates on the subject of nuclear weapons to the effect that American actions, policies, and behavior have little or no influence on the decisions of other nations to acquire nuclear weapons. Some put it this way: What has American restraint ever done for us? It would be simplistic and incorrect to claim that the United States is the prime consideration in every nation's conduct of its security policies. It would be equally foolish to suppose that what the most powerful nation in the world, economically as well as militarily, is doing never enters the mind of a leader trying to calculate his own or his nation's best interests.

It is difficult to calculate the effect of specific American actions on specific countries, and U.S. national policies cannot be calibrated to produce a particular programmed response. But does anyone doubt that raising tariffs or tolerating a fall in the value of the dollar causes some reaction overseas? Can there be any doubt that had the United States decided forty years ago to encourage rather than discourage the spread of nuclear weapons there would be today far more nuclear weapon states than the eight that in fact exist? As to the argument that force, or the threat of its use, is the only language that other nations understand, which is what the question about restraint boils down to: Can anyone doubt that had successive American presidents not shown restraint in the use of America's unparalleled nuclear firepower, other cities would by now have been added to the list that started with Hiroshima and Nagasaki? To all these questions the answer is "No"! U.S. national policies affecting nuclear weapons, including those that guide American actions at home, are as important as international arrangements in influencing the environment of nuclear proliferation.

The military and strategic doctrines of the United States, first of all, should de-emphasize the role of nuclear weapons, limiting it to deterring the use of nuclear weapons by others. There is no real need to declare explicitly (rather than leaving it as implicit) that nuclear weapons could be used against a nation that used biological or chemical weapons against the United States, its forces, or its allies, which was stated in National Security Presidential Directive 17 of September 14, 2002, as quoted in the press:

> The United States will continue to make clear that it reserves the right to respond with overwhelming force—including potentially nuclear weapons—to the use of [weapons of mass destruction] against the United States, our forces abroad and friends and allies.

The United States is powerful enough to retaliate in a devastating way without resorting to nuclear weapons. To threaten their use may enhance the deterrent effect of a determined U.S. military response but it is not a given. Former secretary of state James Baker records in his memoir (*The Politics of Diplomacy*, 1995) that former president George H. W. Bush had decided not to use nuclear weapons in 1991 even if Saddam Hussein had used the chemical weapons he was known to possess. He thought that a threat to remove Hussein from office would deter him from using those weapons of mass destruction. That deterrent did not exist during the 2003 Iraq war because the present Bush administration made Hussein's removal a war aim. But the administration, quite correctly, made clear that any Iraqi officer who authorized the use of chemical or biological weapons would face a war crimes tribunal. This, plus the painfully high cost to the Iraqi leadership and nation that a decision to use these weapons was sure to inflict was a powerful deterrent. In fact, as of this writing, it appears that there were no biological, chemical, or nuclear weapons readily available to Saddam Hussein.

Mixed Signals Regarding Nuclear Weapons

The future role of nuclear weapons has, regrettably, been considerably clouded in the Bush administration's Nuclear Posture Review, which was transmitted with a cover letter from Secretary of Defense Donald Rumsfeld. The text of Rumsfeld's letter speaks of reduced reliance on nuclear weapons and includes the notion of "a credible deterrent at the lowest level of nuclear weapons consistent with the U.S. and allied security." These sentiments are very much in tune with the rollback policy advocated in this book. But the Review sends an ambiguous message about the administration's interpretation of a rollback policy by its endorsement of a need for new designs in the nuclear arsenal:

> Need may arise to modify, upgrade, or replace portions of the extant nuclear force or develop concepts for follow-on nuclear weapons better suited to the nation's needs. It is unlikely that a reduced version of the Cold War nuclear arsenal will be precisely the nuclear force that the United States will require in 2012 and beyond.

A specific need highlighted in the Nuclear Posture Review is for a class of low-yield earth-penetrating nuclear weapons "to defeat emerging threats such as hard and deeply buried targets (HDBT)" of military interest being built in many countries. Among the targets of most concern are very hardened structures—for storing weapons and protecting top-echelon command functions—that are built at depths of 1,000 feet or so with reinforced concrete capable of withstanding up to 1,000 atmospheres overpressure. The actions taken by the United States to address such newly emerging military challenges can, and most likely will, have a major impact on the future of the Non-Proliferation Treaty.

A key technical challenge to destroying such underground targets—in addition to being able to discover exactly where they are located, based on good intelligence information, and to deliver a warhead with precision—is to develop new nuclear weapons that are built strong enough to be able to penetrate into the earth to depths of ten to twenty feet or more without damage before detonating. Detonation at such depths increases the energy of the explosion that is delivered into the ground, instead of into the atmosphere, by a factor of 10 to 20 relative to a surface burst. The warhead therefore hits the target with a much stronger shock, and is more effective as a "bunker buster" than an identical warhead that is detonated on or above the surface. The implication of this is that such penetrating warheads would require much less explosive power to destroy their targets and would therefore cause substantially less collateral damage by reducing the effects of radioactivity and blast. As a consequence it is alleged that these so-called bunker busters would be more acceptable politically and hence more "usable" for attacking buried targets—even in or near urban settings, which are generally preferred locales for such military targets.

It is important to recognize, however, that there are severe limitations on the effectiveness of nuclear bunker busters against HDBTs, and that, unavoidably, they would

produce considerable radioactive debris. These limitations have been determined from extensive experimental
work measuring the depths to which a warhead dropped
from the air and rammed into the earth at a high speed
can maintain its integrity before being detonated; from
known limits on material strengths; and from measure-
ments and calculations of the strength of an explosion that
is required to physically destroy hardened targets of military concern that may be buried at shallow depths, or as
deep as a thousand feet or more. To cite one example,
consider a small nuclear warhead with a yield of one kiloton that is detonated at a depth of fifty feet, which is a
practical limit on penetration into dry hard rock. An explosion of that strength could destroy hardened targets constructed no deeper than two hundred feet below the
surface of the earth. But it would also eject more than one
million cubic feet of radioactive debris from the crater it
would create, about the size of ground zero at the World
Trade Center—bigger than a football field. In order to
avoid creating any crater so as not to disperse fallout into
the atmosphere, such a one-kiloton warhead would itself
need to penetrate to a depth of close to two hundred feet
before exploding. That is physically impossible.

Nuclear weapons are also of limited value against biological and chemical weapons. When detonated underground their effective range in destroying the deadly
effects of pathogens and gases is limited by the fact that
their blast effects extend beyond the area of very high
temperatures and radiation they create for destroying
such agents. Therefore they would be more likely to spread
these agents widely, rather than to destroy them com-

pletely. As an alternative to destroying such localized HDBTs, the United States should pursue effective means to put them out of business—that is, to functionally defeat them—using conventional forces and tactics. This would require improving the ability to locate and seal off their points of access and exit for equipment, resources, and personnel; and, when possible, to establish area control and denial around them.

A decision by the world's only superpower to develop and test new, and presumably "more usable," nuclear weapons for new missions as bunker busters would send a clear and negative signal about the non-proliferation regime to the non-nuclear states. The United States could thereby be dealing a fatal blow to the regime in order to provide itself with a capability of questionable military value.

Moreover, on technical grounds alone, there is no need for the United States to resume testing to develop new nuclear designs for bunker busters. In close to a half century during which it carried out more than 1,000 explosive tests of nuclear devices, the United States has already developed and tested nuclear warheads with a full range of yields from small fractions of a kiloton up to many megatons. The United States can make improvements in their delivery, both in accuracy—using terminal guidance via global positioning satellites (GPS) or laser illumination—and earth penetration—using structurally strengthened warheads. Over many years, the United States has also accumulated an extensive body of data and experience on earth-penetrating munitions. This is an important technology to pursue for many conventional military missions.

The Corrosive Effect of a
Strategy of Unilateral Action

One of the reasons that the United States is not enjoying the broad international support it should have for the campaign against terrorism and proliferation of weapons of mass destruction (nuclear) and terror (biological and chemical) is the perception that unilateral preventive war has become the dominant strain in American thinking about military strategy. The administration can and should change that perception by emphasizing that a continuum of means, of which force and coercion are important components, must be used to deal with the threats posed by such weapons against the security of the United States and its allies. It has begun to do this by pointing out that each case is different and that a policy appropriate for Iraq is not necessarily suitable for North Korea. Multilateral diplomacy, it is saying, is the best medicine for Northeast Asia. In so doing the administration is giving a more balanced emphasis to deterrence and diplomacy as valid tools also to employ in the struggle. Scars remain, however, from the cut and thrust of the campaign to gain support for the Iraq war and it will be important for the White House, as it conducts its anti-proliferation policies, to restore worldwide confidence in the U.S. commitment to cooperation, when that is possible, as its instrument of choice.

V. Achieving Rollback:
The Instruments of Diplomacy

SEVERAL INSTRUMENTS OF diplomacy must be deployed to implement a rollback policy. They include

- Bilateral or regional targeted diplomacy designed to meet the security and other needs of states concerned

- Multilateral or "coalition diplomacy," for example with Russia and others, designed to multiply the influence that the United States alone could bring to bear

- Cooperative threat reduction programs

- Global norms to reinforce the idea of a level playing field, establish standards of expected behavior, and serve as a rallying point for anti-proliferation coalitions

- International organizations to help carry out transparency arrangements and other tasks assigned by the international community

- Coercive diplomacy or enforcement actions when necessary, including military measures as discussed above

Each of these six elements of a coherent U.S. national anti-proliferation policy has been put into practice in the past, but, with changing times, each is in need of being looked at afresh. The connection between military force and statecraft was discussed in a preceding section. The

following sections will review various aspects of the other
instruments of diplomacy.

Targeted Diplomacy

To begin with, if the national security of potential proliferants is a prime driver of their decisions to acquire nuclear
weapons, specifically targeted policies should be adopted
to deal with these concerns. In contrast to the United
States' viewing each proliferant simply as a security problem—as a nuisance at best and possibly as a dangerous
enemy—such a targeted approach would offer the option
of actually trying to respond to the specific issues that are
motivating potential proliferants. In the end, this obser-
vation applies to all nations, but it applies with special
force to de facto or undeclared nuclear weapon states like
India, Pakistan, and Israel, which have very real and
immediate needs that must be satisfied in some way if they
are even to contemplate joining in a rollback program.
The point is, of course, immediately relevant to the conduct of diplomacy with North Korea and Iran.

The Bush administration's "National Strategy to Combat Weapons of Mass Destruction" (December 2002) spoke
of "targeted strategies against proliferants." Why not
think, as well, of "targeted strategies pursued jointly with
proliferants"—that is, strategies that would employ cooperative as well as confrontational methods to head off
nuclear proliferation? Cooperation between adversaries
was possible during the Cold War between the Soviet
Union and the United States. It should be possible in other
cases now.

It has been clear for some time, to cite one example,

that North Korea has genuine security concerns stemming, in part, from its own antagonistic policies toward its neighbors and toward the United States, and that its leaders are mainly interested in survival of the regime. The United States, like its ally South Korea, should be interested in societal change in North Korea as the best way to improve the lot of the Koreans who live in the North and to bring about changes in state behavior. U.S. policy has veered between engagement and ostracism as ways to achieve that, when the United States thinks about North Korea at all. North Korea is not a state aiming at global or even regional domination. And it is conceivable that a U.S. effort, sustained and high-level, could inaugurate a process of cooperation leading to a resolution of the issues that have festered in the Korean peninsula since the end of the Korean War in 1953. Only in that context is it likely that, short of war, the persistent problem of nuclear proliferation will be solved. The solution will require a mix of cooperation and strong pressure—not all one or the other.

It may be necessary to arrange stronger security assurances to nations that enter into a united effort against nuclear proliferation and voluntarily forgo the acquisition of nuclear weapons. "Negative assurances" already are provided, which oblige the nuclear weapon states to refrain from using nuclear weapons against any non–nuclear weapon state that is a signatory of the Non-Proliferation Treaty. Never viewed as very reassuring, these assurances have been eroded by a public and explicit emphasis by the United States on using nuclear weapons in response to the use of biological or chemical weapons by non–nuclear weapon states. New assurances should include provisions that offer more ironclad guarantees concerning their sovereignty and territorial integrity. Those provided to Ukraine in the context of its giving up nuclear weapons might be taken as a model. There should also be increasing support for regional treaties in order to assure the total absence of nuclear weapons in their respective territories (Article VII of the NPT). To the several nuclear-free zones already established, it would be desirable to add a Central Asian Nuclear Free Zone, a subject already under discussion.

Economic and trade benefits, especially in the area of energy supplies, should be negotiated as tangible benefits for nations that join in the effort to create and maintain an effective anti-proliferation regime. Economic incentives should add to the attraction to them of selecting national policies that would enhance their security without resorting to the development of nuclear weapons. Such policies should address any perceived damage to their economic health arising from their obeying trade restraints in their support of the Non-Proliferation Treaty. As guaranteed in Article IV of the Non-Proliferation Treaty, parties should reap the benefits from nuclear energy for peaceful purposes and, with proper inspections, should be able to develop the facilities and carry out the research and development necessary to achieve the medical and energy benefits of nuclear technology. But the signatories must also enforce trade restrictions on equipment useful for building nuclear weapons, and allow a broad right of review of dual-purpose technologies and facilities.

Diplomatic moves to respond to security concerns of potential proliferants, it should be noted, must include strenuous efforts to resolve regional disputes and tensions that generate specific requirements for powerful military forces. On some occasions, when and where appropriate, those requirements should be met by the provision of conventional weapons by the United States and its allies, or by the insertion of peacekeeping forces.

U.S.-Russia Responsibilities

Coalition diplomacy is necessary to present potential proliferants with a united front in opposition to their nuclear ambitions. In this effort, U.S.-Russian cooperation must play a central role. These two countries—by far the two largest nuclear weapon states—have the capacity either to undermine each other's attempts to roll back proliferation or to make their attempts mutually reinforcing.

A blueprint already is in place for cooperative efforts. It is called the Declaration of Moscow, signed by Presidents Bush and Putin in May 2002. Implementation of the commitments recorded in that document would be of enormous help in rolling back nuclear proliferation. Particularly important would be an increase in the amount of weapons-usable fissile material to be eliminated or placed in internationally monitored secure storage. Presidential attention will be required to overcome current barriers holding up progress on technical issues. It is needed now.

In their joint Declaration of Moscow, President Bush and President Putin called on all nations to strengthen and strictly enforce export controls, interdict illegal transfers, prosecute violators, and tighten border controls to prevent and protect against the proliferation of biological and chemical, as well as nuclear weapons. The importance of this cooperation was made very clear by the joint action by the United States and Russia in 2002 to remove inadequately protected nuclear material located in Yugoslavia.

The scope of the agenda, and the spirit displayed in this Joint Declaration by Presidents Bush and Putin, provide a good basis for cooperative efforts to strengthen the nuclear non-proliferation regime. The United States and Russia are the possessors of more than 90 percent of all the nuclear weapons in the world and their leadership in moving toward a world of cooperation rather than confrontation is vitally important to sending the right message to other countries.

It is important to show that the two nations are drastically reducing their reliance on nuclear weapons. The Bush-Putin summit meeting in Moscow in May 2002 resulted in a treaty—denoted the Treaty of Moscow, or Strategic Offensive Reductions Treaty (SORT)—to reduce the number of warheads to remain deployed by each on their operational strategic offensive forces to 1,700–2,200 by the year 2012. Consent to the ratification of that treaty has been given by the U.S. Senate, with conditions that strengthen it, and also by the Russian State Duma. It formally entered into force in June 2003.

The very existence of such a treaty negotiated by the two countries within an agreed framework of cooperation is far more important than whether the number of operationally deployed warheads should have been 1,000 or 2,000 or whether the implementation date should have been 2007 or 2012. It is to be regretted, however, that the Treaty provisions are silent concerning the dismantling of non-deployed nuclear bombs and warheads. And so the United States and Russia can each, if they wish to, maintain a much larger arsenal of some 7,000 to 8,000 warheads for long-range strategic delivery systems, including warheads held in reserve. The primary impact of the treaty is to reduce the number of deployed warheads by downloading rather than destroying them. Hence there will be many more warheads and much more bomb material—uranium and plutonium—in Russia, and also in the United States, which could fall into dangerous hands. This is a major flaw—unnecessary as well as unwelcome.

There is no plausible reason for the United States and Russia each to maintain 8,000 warheads when it is remembered that just one bomb, whose yield was a little more than what might be a trigger in today's modern weapons, destroyed the entire city of Hiroshima. If each side maintained 8,000 warheads, the total number would add up to more than ten times the number of warheads possessed by all other six nuclear nations combined. That large number, if no irreversible steps are taken toward reducing it, will not help in achieving anti-proliferation goals.

In a regrettable retreat from the START II Treaty, which will now never be ratified, the Treaty of Moscow permits the United States and Russia to retain land-based ICBMs with multiple independently targetable reentry vehicles (MIRVs). This failure to rid the world of monster land-based ballistic missiles with many warheads, like the ten-warhead MIRVd SS18 or newer designs now being built and deployed, perpetuates the threat they pose as accurate first-strike weapons, each one of which is capable of destroying a number of an adversary's silo-based missiles. The threat to stability of such missiles in the new U.S. relationship with Russia is not the same as it was during the Cold War, but extending the service life of such destructive weapons, particularly under circumstances where Russia's early warning system is not as capable as it should be, is a risky proposition.

An additional concern is the vagueness of the Treaty of Moscow as regards implementation. This is what the U.S. Senate sought to repair with the conditions, which dealt with Nunn-Lugar funding and annual estimates of force levels, that it attached to its resolution of ratification. In order to avoid confusion and allegations of noncompliance, the Bilateral Implementation Commission, to be established under Article III of the Treaty, also must provide a mechanism to clear up and settle compliance issues relating to the definition of "strategic warheads," to counting active vs. deactivated warheads, to setting verification standards, and to settling issues of force reconstitution before these issues become causes of friction. The U.S. Senate appears to be well aware of these problems.

The U.S. Senate's conditions and declarations attached to its resolution of ratification of the Treaty of Moscow show clearly that there is strong bipartisan support in the Senate for U.S.-Russian cooperation in putting their nuclear competition behind them. This support should strengthen the hands of the U.S. and Russian administrations in reducing the salience of nuclear weapons in their relationship, and in reducing the total number of warheads. Even though neither the Treaty nor the Declaration of Moscow provides for dismantling warheads or delivery systems, the U.S. Senate has shown its support for this in very strong terms.

There are economic as well as arms control reasons for further reductions in the large force of non–operationally deployed nuclear warheads planned for retention by the Bush administration and by Russia. To maintain a larger nuclear infrastructure and build a larger pit-manufacturing capacity would require the United States to spend a lot more money. Here is an example of the impact: research during the past five years under the U.S. Department of Energy's Stockpile Stewardship Program has taught the U.S. weapons community a great deal about the behavior of plutonium, one of the most difficult and idiosyncratic metals, a reactor-made product that is the fuel for most nuclear weapons. Research on the effect of aging on the crystal structure of plutonium has shown that the nuclear pits in the warheads can be expected to retain their effectiveness for 50–60 years or longer. To maintain an arsenal of 2,000 pits, if they live 50 years or more, would require an ability to produce approximately 40 new pits a year as replacements. This can be accommodated at the Los Alamos National Laboratory, but if the total warhead number remains at close to current levels of about 8,000, instead of just the 2,000 to be deployed, facilities for manufacturing more than 160 pits per year would be required. This would require the United States to build and operate a major new multibillion dollar facility.

Part of the process of escaping from the mutual deterrence trap should be an attempt by Russia and the United States to cooperate in building and operating suitable defensive programs, as well as continuing to dismantle offensive nuclear weapons. To begin with, the United States should assist Russia in building a modern satellite-based early warning system for detecting attacks against its homeland. The United States has used infrared sensors aboard the Defense Support Program (DSP) satellites for many years for early warning of a missile attack. By all

accounts a more primitive Russian early warning system
is in poor operational status, and does not provide early
warning from all directions of approach to Russia. U.S.
cooperation and support, including joint operations, could
greatly enhance Russia's confidence in getting early warning of a missile attack. The technology for such a system
is widely available and sharing it would in no way compromise U.S. security. This issue is addressed in a later
section of this book. The next step, consistent with the
Bush-Putin Declaration of May 2002, would be to develop
and, if technically useful, deploy national and Europe-oriented ballistic missile defenses. U.S.-Russian cooperation
could be a model, in some respects, for U.S. cooperation
with other nations.

Beyond the technical challenges of ballistic missile
defense, there are some important strategic and political
issues in the U.S.-Russia context that need to be weighed
in making decisions as to exactly how the United States
should pursue its missile defense program. It is essential
for the two nations to preserve an element of predictability
in their military relationship. The Joint Declaration of
Moscow had it right in stating that:

> The United States and Russia have also agreed to study
> possible areas for missile defense cooperation, includ-
> ing the expansion of joint exercises related to missile
> defense, and the exploration of potential programs for
> the joint research and development of missile defense
> technologies, bearing in mind the importance of the
> mutual protection of classified information and the safe-
> guarding of intellectual property rights.

Those words, in fact, hark back to President Reagan's
policies on ballistic missile defense. Measures of cooper-

ation and transparency in the area of missile defense as called for in the Bush-Putin Declaration, including the exchange of information on missile defense programs and tests, and reciprocal visits to observe the tests and operations to improve familiarity, should be implemented. Unfortunately, there are no tangible signs of this at present. Indeed, a shroud of secrecy has now enveloped the U.S. ballistic missile defense program so tightly that its plans and the results of any of the actual test flights have become well hidden from the American public.

Beyond its general statements, the Joint Declaration by the U.S. and Russian leaders established a Consultative Group for Strategic Security (CGSS) to be chaired by foreign ministers and defense ministers, with the participation of other senior officials. The CGSS provides operational content to the agreement with this mission statement:

> This group will be the principal mechanism through which the sides strengthen mutual confidence, expand transparency, share information and plans, and discuss strategic issues of mutual interest.

As a general statement of principles this is really significant. The test of its value will come in facing the devil in the details of implementation—including for starters, getting the Consultative Group to operate as a problem-solving mechanism on a continuous basis, something that will require a dedicated, full-time staff.

Cooperative Threat Reduction

To make the existing bulwarks of the non-proliferation regime more effective, the Nunn-Lugar Cooperative

Threat Reduction Program should be extended to apply on a global basis. So far, the United States has focused its efforts on the countries of the former Soviet Union, which have been repositories of the largest stockpiles of nuclear fuel and weapons. This work, initiated in 1992, has contributed significantly to improving safeguards of this dangerous material against spreading into dangerous hands. Although much has been accomplished, more than half of this material in the former Soviet Union still remains to be protected with improved security. The Harvard Project on Managing the Atom (see page 21) estimates that less than 40 percent of the more than a thousand tons of special nuclear material—that is, material that can be used as fuel for nuclear weapons—in the former Soviet Union has been given "rapid upgrade," and less than half of that has been secured with "comprehensive" protection. A senior bipartisan group led by former senator Howard Baker and former White House counsel Lloyd Cutler in their 2001 report for the Department of Energy, titled "A Report Card on the Department of Energy's Non-Proliferation Programs with Russia," wrote:

> The most urgent unmet national security threat to the United States today is the danger that weapons of mass destruction or weapons usable material in Russia could be stolen and sold to terrorists or hostile nation states.

Three major recommendations of this panel are (1) this threat to the United States should be designated as top priority; (2) a strategic plan for addressing it as rapidly as practical should be put in place; and (3) a senior official at the White House level in the United States should be put in charge of carrying it out.

To implement these recommendations the Baker-Cutler panel recommended that more resources be provided than at the current level. In rough numbers the United States contributes $1 billion per year and is committed to do so for the next ten years, with a slight funding increase to include work on securing chemical and biological weapons. Roughly two-thirds of that amount is devoted to programs relating to managing nuclear weapons material and expertise. The Department of Energy supports the material protection, control, and accountability program for special nuclear material and the Department of Defense has the responsibility for the nuclear weapons protection part of the program. Smaller grants from the international community are awarded to individual scientists to keep them active and engaged in productive scientific civilian research as an alternative to selling their expertise to would-be proliferators in other nations around the world. In addition to this support, the non-U.S. members of the Group of Eight (G8) have committed collectively to add $10 billion to the effort to supplement $10 billion provided by the United States over the next decade. Known as the "Global Partnership Against the Spread of Weapons of Mass Destruction," it now includes nations beyond the G8 who also have pledged to make contributions.

Most of that amount has recently been confirmed in the form of national pledges, although unfortunately there is now a tendency to view the pledges as ceilings, rather than floors. The Senior Officials Group of the G8 reported to the G8 Summit at their June 2–3, 2003, meeting in Evian, France, that this collective commitment has been translated into firm national commitments over ten years of up to: United States, $10 billion; Germany, 1.5 billion euros; United Kingdom, $750 million; France, 750 million euros; Japan, $200 million; Italy, 1 billion euros; Canada, Can$1 billion. The European Union has pledged 1 billion euros and Russia $2 billion. Finland, Norway, Poland, Sweden, and Switzerland have indicated their interest in joining the Global Partnership as donors. The G8 also agreed to improve the security of radioactive materials in order to reduce the threat of radiological weapons, or the so-called "dirty bombs." In particular, the G8 will identify elements of the IAEA's Code of Conduct on the Safety and Security of Radioactive Sources that are of the greatest relevance to preventing terrorists or states that harbor them from gaining access to high-risk radioactive sources, and will consider developing recommendations on how those elements could be applied at the national level.

These are encouraging developments, but they should be seen in the context of the Baker-Cutler recommendation, which is that the annual funding authorized by the United States Congress should be tripled to $3 billion, still less than 1 percent of the U.S. national defense spending, and, when translated into G8 terms, far more than the Global Partnership Program is contemplating.

Specific actions for strengthening the Nunn-Lugar Cooperative Threat Reduction program should start with a stronger vote of confidence by the U.S. government in the program with steady financial support increased to the levels recommended by the Baker-Cutler panel. In addition, steps should be taken to expand technical cooperation in sensors and methods for physically protecting both the weapons and material using the best technologies, and to improve transparency to assure that all weapons-usable fissile material is stored properly. This work might also include collaborative research and development on advancing proliferation-resistant nuclear technologies that could be made available under IAEA monitoring to other countries for peaceful purposes.

Global Norms: The Non-Proliferation Treaty

Global norms help to establish an anti-proliferation regime among all responsible nations of the world. A challenge raised frequently is: "But what value are such norms if rogue states or terrorists ignore and flout them?" Their value is in enabling coalitions of responsible nations opposing proliferation to be formed. Without this aura of legitimacy and shared expectations that nuclear proliferation should be opposed, it would be more difficult to assemble international support for anti-proliferation actions.

President Bush has subscribed to a requirement to bolster the nuclear non-proliferation treaty (NPT), both in the Declaration of Moscow and in his administration's "National Strategy to Combat Weapons of Mass Destruction." The latter document commits the Bush administration to working to improve compliance with the NPT. There are some voices of despair who say that the non-proliferation regime has failed. In fact, that regime has been highly successful, as noted earlier, measured by the small number of nuclear weapon states that exist and by the number of states that turned away from programs or actual possession of nuclear weapons. It can be even more successful if rollback is adopted as the U.S. strategy in this field.

The Non-Proliferation Treaty, which was signed in 1968 and entered into force in 1970, stands as a major success of the patient application of diplomacy. Its five-year treaty review cycles have helped to forge anti-proliferation coalitions. In very broad terms the regime is designed (1) to prevent the spread of nuclear weapons; (2) to provide assurance through international safeguards that the peaceful nuclear activities of states that have not already developed nuclear weapons will not and cannot be diverted to making such weapons; (3) to promote, to the maximum extent consistent with other purposes of this treaty, the peaceful uses of nuclear energy by non-nuclear weapon parties under appropriate international safeguards; and (4) to express the determination of the parties that the treaty should lead to further progress in comprehensive arms control and toward nuclear disarmament in the long term, the famous Article VI of the treaty. All but four countries in the world—India, Israel, Pakistan, and North Korea, which withdrew recently—are formally committed to NPT. As noted earlier, during the decades since Hiroshima and Nagasaki a significant number of nations that had started down the road to nuclear weapons abandoned them.

Global Norms:
The Comprehensive Test Ban Treaty

Another, and related regime, also is in place: so far as is known, the only nuclear test explosions that have occurred since the Comprehensive Test Ban Treaty was opened for signature on September 24, 1996, were those conducted by India and Pakistan, and those nations themselves have

not tested in five years. The United States has not conducted a test explosion since 1992. Nuclear weapons tests
may not be essential for states determined to build simple,
first-generation nuclear weapons, but they are necessary
for states that intend to develop more advanced or mature
nuclear weapons capabilities. A ban on such tests provides
a strong reinforcing mechanism for the NPT and helps to
assure compliance with it.

Many nations signed on to the indefinite extension of
the NPT in 1995 on the explicit condition that the nuclear
powers would cease all nuclear-yield testing. This situation presented the United States and the other nuclear
powers with a strong political and strategic incentive to
formalize the moratorium on testing by ratifying and
working to bring into force the Comprehensive Test Ban
Treaty (CTBT) signed by the United States in 1996. It is
obviously one of the critical cornerstones of the NPT,
which, as Secretary Colin Powell said in his testimony
before the Senate Foreign Relations Committee on July 9,
2002, "is the centerpiece of the global non-proliferation
regime." A U.S. decision to resume testing to produce new
nuclear weapons would therefore dramatically undermine the NPT. Conversely, a U.S. decision to ratify the
already signed CTBT and lead the effort to bring the treaty
into force would be an effective way of strengthening the
NPT and, through it, worldwide anti-proliferation efforts.

Bringing the treaty into force would have the added
technical advantage of allowing for the full implementation of the verification system described in the treaty to
verify compliance. Full implementation would add to the
worldwide remote-monitoring network a challenge-
inspection protocol that would permit on-site inspections

of suspicious events. Currently, the Bush administration has declined to participate in the on-going work in Vienna to develop the on-site inspection regime and is refusing to fund the U.S. share of that activity. All U.S. allies in NATO, including Great Britain, Germany, and France, have signed and ratified the CTBT, as have Japan and Russia. Israel has signed the CTBT and is participating energetically in the work of setting up a verification system. Others, including China, have indicated they will work to bring the treaty into force once the United States has ratified it. As of May 2003, 31 of the 44 states that have built nuclear reactors, the so-called "nuclear-capable states," that must ratify the treaty for it to enter into force, have done so. In all, 97 states have ratified and 166 have signed. It is time for the United States to reconsider the issue of ratifying the CTBT. The White House and the Senate should enter into a serious debate to clarify the underlying issues, both the concerns and opportunities. This debate was not adequately joined in 1999 when the CTBT first came before the Senate for its advice and consent to ratification, and regrettably the Bush administration has thus far refused to reopen the question.

Why is the United States reluctant? In addition to the dubious need to develop "concepts for follow-on nuclear weapons better suited to the nation's needs," including nuclear earth penetrators against HDBTs, opponents of the CTBT have raised two questions: (1) "How can we be sure that many years ahead, we will not need to resume yield testing in order to rebuild the stockpile?"; and (2) "How can we monitor compliance by other CTBT signatories to standards consistent with U.S. national security?"

The answer to the first question is that total certainty

can never be achieved. But it is possible to ensure that there is a strong program in place with the necessary support of competent engineers and scientists who would sound a warning bell should a serious, unforeseen problem arise. With the enhanced, multifaceted, science-based program of stockpile stewardship established during the past eight years, the United States can have confidence in its ability to understand the character of the stockpile and the way in which special bomb materials age. As a result of the stockpile surveillance program, a number of flaws have been reported and dealt with appropriately. The flaws thus far uncovered within the nuclear devices themselves are related primarily to design oversights. That is, the flaws, or their precursors, were present when the weapons were put into the stockpile.

The United States can be assured that the CTBT is consistent with the ability to retain high confidence in the reliability of its existing nuclear force for decades. This conclusion has been demonstrated convincingly by a number of detailed technical analyses. In 1995 a team of independent scientists working with colleagues from the weapons community, including technical leaders involved in creating the current nuclear arsenal, reached this finding (Nuclear Testing; JASON 1995 report for the Department of Energy). It was that determination that led the United States to negotiate the CTBT and sign it in 1996. Most recently, in August 2002, a panel of the National Academy of Sciences published a comprehensive study on Technical Issues Related to the Comprehensive Test Bam Treaty. The study group, which included retired directors of weapons laboratories, bomb designers, and technical and scientific experts, concluded that the United States can

maintain confidence in its enduring stockpile under a ban
on all nuclear-yield testing, provided it has a well-sup-
ported, science-based stewardship and maintenance program, together with a capability to remanufacture
warheads as needed.

A similar detailed analysis that addressed strategic as
well as technical issues, led by General John M. Shalikashvili, former chairman of the Joint Chiefs of Staff, was conducted in 2000–2001 with government cooperation and
authorization and it reached the same conclusion. In his
letter to the President, General Shalikashvili affirmed that
the CTBT "is a very important part of global non-proliferation efforts and is compatible with keeping a safe, reli-
able U.S. nuclear deterrent."

Concerning the question of compliance, there is broad
agreement that the United States could monitor CTBT
compliance to standards consistent with its national security. Based on its technical analysis, the National Academy
of Sciences study group concluded that

> The worst-case scenario under a no-CTBT regime poses
> far bigger threats to U.S. security—sophisticated
> nuclear weapons in the hands of many more adversar-
> ies—than the worst-case scenario of clandestine testing
> in a CTBT regime, within the constraints posed by the
> monitoring system.

As noted by General Shalikashvili in his study, "Ironically
the more testing expertise a country has, the better able it
would be to conduct an evasive test and extract useful
information—but the less difference that information
would probably make in advancing the country's nuclear
capabilities." Conversely, it is true that the less experience

in nuclear weapons that a country has, the more difficult it is to carry out successfully a useful test without actually exceeding the low detection threshold of the fully implemented verification system.

When fully implemented under a CTBT, the verification system becomes more robust and difficult to evade, since it will then acquire challenge rights to check out data initially derived from remote sensors by conducting short-notice, on-site inspections of suspicious events. For a very modest cost, the international monitoring network could be improved—for example, by incorporating private or government seismic stations as full-time participants in the detection system. A further strengthening of the sensitivity of the CTBT to detect covert, treaty-violating activities could be negotiated by adding appropriate bilateral transparency and confidence-building measures with the other nuclear powers, Russia and China in particular. These would permit on-site sensors to be introduced at their instrumented test sites to monitor for signals—seismic and radiological—from possible underground tests that are banned by the CTBT. The Bush administration should clearly state its willingness to initiate such an arrangement, reciprocally with the Russians, at Novaya Zemlya and the Nevada Test Site. Bilateral forums that supplement, but cooperate with, the existing CTBT organization would be needed to manage this process.

The CTBT does not increase the requirements for the United States to monitor and identify underground testing. The United States will want all information on testing activities, with or without the treaty. It does, however, add to the difficulties for a country to evade the treaty not only by strengthening the system but also by adding the inspection rights. Furthermore, given that the United States has the most advanced and sophisticated diagnostic, analytical, experimental, and computation facilities, it is in a stronger position than other nations to maintain a deterrent under a test ban. As General Shalikashvili concluded in his study, "I believe that an objective and thorough net assessment shows convincingly that U.S. interests, as well as those of friends and allies, will be served by the Treaty's entry into force."

Pending entry into force, the United States should do whatever it takes to strengthen the present moratorium, which has now lasted eleven years. This would involve stronger statements of no intention to resume nuclear testing than the administration has yet made. And it would include stronger support for the International Monitoring System (IMS) that the treaty has established, components of which already exist. The administration should continue to support the IMS financially and also begin to fund the development of the on-site inspection regime so that it could be implemented voluntarily even before the treaty enters into force. It also should facilitate the addition of seismic research stations to the network, as mentioned earlier, and try to supplement them with bilateral monitoring agreements with other nuclear weapon states, especially China and Russia. Without question, the United States should maintain and strengthen existing national technical capabilities for verifying treaty compliance.

Building New Regimes: Avoiding Miscalculation and Strengthening Defense Cooperation

As noted earlier, the security environment of the future may include crises in which more than two nuclear weapon states are involved and thus may pose greater uncertainty about the origins and intent of nuclear explosions. Worst-case planning and worst-case assumptions generally promote tensions and reduce the opportunities for cooperation. More effective early warning systems could help with these problems. As also noted earlier, the technology required for such systems is widely available and has existed for many years. Sharing it would in no way compromise U.S. security on technical grounds. On strategic grounds, the stability that such a system would enhance for many countries against the fear of surprise attack would contribute to security worldwide, including that of the United States.

Would countries other than Russia, and perhaps some U.S. allies, be interested in early warning cooperation as a first step toward even deeper military cooperation? The specific answer, of course, would be different for each country and would depend, in part, on the levels of technical expertise in this area possessed by individual countries. Related factors include receptivity to transparency in fairly sensitive security areas and the availability of funding. Political questions, such as the nature of the relations between potentially cooperating states and perceptions regarding the purposes of early warning cooperation, also would be important.

In general, the purpose of early warning cooperation would be to reduce or eliminate miscalculations by providing a more accurate picture of what is happening and extra minutes of time for threat assessment; to minimize incentives for prompt launch procedures; and to support national decisions to keep offensive nuclear forces at the lowest levels judged necessary for security. The support for these objectives should be fairly widespread.

The first steps in setting up programs of cooperation in early warning should consist of bilateral talks between the United States and potential participants, with the exception of the NATO countries where multilateral forums already exist. If a series of bilateral programs of cooperation were established, some method of creating transparency among the programs should be developed to minimize suspicion and to help the learning process.

There would be political and security benefits from multinational cooperation. They include

- Building a coalition of nations whose enemies would be seen to be rogue states and terrorist organizations, not each other

- Creating conditions conducive to mutual restraint in strategic matters generally

- Developing a forum for coordinating anti-proliferation activities and presenting a common front against nuclear proliferation

- Facilitating a harmonized response to the use by any nation or terrorist group of any type of weapon of mass destruction or terror

Anti-proliferation coalitions should not, of course, be limited to nuclear weapon states. Those major nations that have renounced the acquisition of nuclear weapons, even though they have all the ingredients for producing robust nuclear weapons arsenals, also should be included. This would include Germany, Japan, South Korea, South Africa, Argentina, Brazil, Sweden, Canada, Australia, Ukraine, and probably one of the leading states of the Middle East, of which Iran would be the best choice.

International Organizations:
The International Atomic Energy Agency

Nations require international organizations to carry on some of the work they want done in the external realm. Such organizations are not independent entities, as some critics of them mistakenly believe. Rather they are servants of their member states, delegated to carry out certain well-defined functions assigned to them. This is the case regarding the international organizations created to help monitor treaties dealing with deadly weapons, for example, the CTBT and the chemical weapons convention. The International Atomic Energy Agency (IAEA) looms very large in nuclear non-proliferation matters because it was assigned responsibility for monitoring certain aspects of the nuclear Non-Proliferation Treaty (NPT).

Unfortunately, in the international climate that existed nearly forty years ago when the NPT was being negotiated, the IAEA had only token inspection responsibilities. Its main task was to confirm that no nuclear materials diversions were taking place from nuclear facilities being assisted by nuclear weapon states. When the NPT came into effect, the IAEA was asked to monitor all nuclear activities of the non–nuclear weapon states, but its access was limited to those facilities declared by those states.

Although the statute of the IAEA could be interpreted as permitting very broad inspection rights and responsibilities, the Board of Governors of the IAEA, an agent of the member states, never could agree that the Agency should exercise those rights and responsibilities. The IAEA was not empowered to look for undeclared facilities. That climate of low expectations began to change in the 1990s when the IAEA was asked to monitor North Korea's nuclear facilities. The then director-general of the IAEA, Dr. Hans Blix, having been burned by the revelations of undeclared nuclear activities in Iraq, already had decided to ask for more authority to inspect undeclared suspect sites. That authority still has not been granted by all the member states as of this writing.

In 2002, it was learned that the North Koreans had not just one, but two weapons development programs, the visible one designed to build a plutonium bomb and the covert one designed to enrich natural uranium for an HEU bomb. And Iran is engaged in building a large gas centrifuge facility for the enrichment of uranium, presumably for use as bomb material. These developments underscore the importance of expanding the authority of the IAEA for verifying compliance with the provisions of the Non-Proliferation Treaty. The Bush administration has proposed that the IAEA Additional Protocol, which gives the IAEA more authority for monitoring, should be generally accepted. This is the right point to make, but unless aggressive moves are made to accomplish this, the Additional Protocol will not be applied in the most critical cases. Its value, and the effectiveness of IAEA in preventing proliferation, would be further strengthened by a UN agreement to prohibit plutonium reprocessing facilities and uranium enrichment plants from being included as components of the nuclear infrastructure of non-nuclear weapon states.

The U.S. administration also has called for "appropriate increase in funding" for the IAEA. This is certainly necessary, for the IAEA has been starved of funding for years. Probably, the administration will have to campaign among other IAEA member states to change the situation, as well as put more money into its own FY2004 budget.

The Non-Proliferation Treaty requires those non-nuclear weapon states that have subscribed to its provisions to negotiate a Safeguards Agreement with the IAEA. The Safeguards Agreement that is in effect with many adherents to the NPT dates back some years and does not include the access rights that most experts now believe are necessary to monitor undeclared nuclear facilities. This is why it is so essential for the Additional Protocol to be applied as soon as possible.

There should be a deadline declared by the Board of Governors of the IAEA, or by the UN Security Council, for states to conclude an agreement with the IAEA to put into effect the provisions of the Additional Protocol. After that date, states that have not accepted it would be denied nuclear-related assistance. Similar penalties, as appropriate, would be applied to those states, like India and Pakistan, nonadherents to the NPT, that assist other nations that have not accepted the Additional Protocol after the deadline declared by the IAEA or the UN Security Council.

The UN Security Council should undertake the task of enforcing the inspection provisions of the IAEA, including those penalties to be imposed in the event of non-adherence to the Additional Protocol, or in the event of assistance being provided to another state to develop nuclear weapons by a non-adherent to the NPT, or in the event of a refusal by a state to accept inspections requested by the IAEA. Enforcing these essential elements of an effective anti-proliferation program may require the authorization of military force by the UN Security Council, including the use of force to impose an inspection that has been declared necessary by the IAEA and endorsed by the UN Security Council.

The nuclear weapon states, all members of the IAEA, also could give the Agency more responsibilities regarding their own nuclear-weapons related activities. The IAEA, for example, may have a shared responsibility, with the United States and Russia, for monitoring dismantled nuclear warheads stored at the Mayak facility constructed with Nunn-Lugar assistance near Chelyabinsk in the Urals. It is also possible to think of an IAEA responsibility for some aspects of the supplemental nuclear test monitoring system for Russia, China, and the United States mentioned previously.

Finally, the IAEA could be assigned a larger role in collecting data concerning transfers of nuclear materials and equipment. Member states should be asked to register all such transfers, receiving as well as shipping, with the IAEA on a regular basis. The Nuclear Suppliers Group also should be requested to file reports with the IAEA, although not the details of all its deliberations.

Such actions would strengthen the capabilities for verifying the NPT. This would not only provide greater confidence in compliance with its provisions by all signatories but also answer those in the United States and elsewhere who doubt the durability and continuing value of the current non-proliferation regime. As noted earlier, George Tenet, Director of Central Intelligence, questioned the prospects of continuing the present non-proliferation regime in his report to the Senate on February 11, 2003, when he said, "We have entered a new world of proliferation," observing that "more has changed on proliferation over the past year than any other issue." His concern and pessimism about maintaining the non-proliferation regime in the future centered on those "non-state purveyors"—that is, private companies or, in some cases, individuals, who are making technology and equipment available to potential nuclear proliferants for cash. Such sources are increasingly able to provide the technology and equipment that previously could only be supplied by countries with established nuclear capabilities.

Director Tenet's remarks emphasize the importance of greatly strengthening the means of verifying such activities. This will require broad international cooperation in monitoring commerce and illegal trafficking in nuclear materials in the years ahead. The complexities that have multiplied and the increasingly brazen challenges that have been flung at the international community are sufficiently alarming to make this issue one that should be given the highest priority by the U.S. government. A vigorous diplomatic campaign must be carried forward with the necessary resources. If that is done, there is every hope that this generation of American leaders can do as well as those who established a non-proliferation regime during the most threatening conditions throughout the Cold War years and bequeathed this nation a world with only eight nuclear weapon states.

There is evidently great urgency in enlarging the authority of IAEA and backing it with the enforcement responsibilities of the United Nations Security Council in matters of verifying compliance with the Non-Proliferation Treaty. This will be necessary if this regime is to have any real hope of surviving into the future. And until someone can come up with a better model for reducing nuclear danger, the nations of the world have no better alternative than to make this system work, no matter how difficult and protracted the effort may be.

VI. Applying Recommended Policies to Specific Cases

IN THE PRECEDING discussion a broad and strengthened anti-proliferation policy has been outlined, based on the principles of rolling back nascent nuclear weapons capabilities and scaling back the nuclear weapons holdings of declared nuclear weapon states, relying heavily on diplomatic tools backed up by military strength. The following discussion addresses the question of how those principles and other recommendations offered in this book might be applied in specific cases. The cases to be examined are China, North Korea, Iran, Israel, India and Pakistan. In each case, a multilateral context will be essential to the success of anti-proliferation policies.

Very frequently, in the history of U.S. non-proliferation diplomacy, there has been a tendency to focus on the single issue of nuclear weapons and to ignore all the other aspects of the relationship. Ukraine, seen by the United States almost exclusively in non-proliferation terms in 1992, was a case in point, and North Korea is too. Iran comes close to that situation, and India and Pakistan received that treatment for awhile. Now, the pendulum has swung too far in the opposite direction as regards India and Pakistan, and U.S. policy has only rarely addressed the potential of a positive contribution to non-proliferation by Israel. Because the potential proliferant makes security decisions in a broader context than non-proliferation considerations, the United States also should deal with the issue in a broad strategic context.

The discussion below describes policies that the United States should pursue within such a context.

China

As one of the nuclear weapon states, as so defined in the nuclear Non-Proliferation Treaty, China shares the responsibilities assigned to nuclear weapon states by the treaty. China's record regarding transfers of nuclear materials and technology in recent years has been good. However, China gave Pakistan considerable help in establishing that country's nuclear weapons program. It was also somewhat lax in earlier years before tightening its controls over exports of missile-related technology.

"Scale-back," rather than "rollback," is the way to think about China's own nuclear forces. This refers in particular to its short-range missiles and to possible future plans for modernizing and expanding its long-range ballistic missiles. The continuing deployment of short-range, though conventionally armed, ballistic missiles opposite Taiwan, for example, is an incitement to an arms race as well as a destabilizing element in East Asia. So far, China has been quite restrained in its deployment of intercontinental ballistic missiles (ICBMs); this nuclear force consists of some two dozen missiles, none in a high state of readiness. The future may be a different story.

China probably could build up its long-range nuclear forces quite rapidly, given its strong economy and available technology. Some forecasts anticipate a force of mobile ICBMs, armed with several hundred multiple, independently targetable reentry vehicles (MIRVs). This would be a formidable force and it would challenge India to build up its forces. The situation also would raise concerns in Japan, Pakistan, and the Korean Peninsula. China's decisions about its future nuclear forces will play a key role in efforts to prevent a nuclear arms race in Asia, and to combat the spread of nuclear weapons to additional nations and to terrorist groups.

U.S. actions and policies inevitably will be key factors in what China does. If the United States describes China as a potential peer adversary, as was the case at an early stage in the current Bush administration, the Chinese will react accordingly. They may, anyway, since their aspirations probably include becoming a global military power at some stage. But there is no point in egging them on.

The ongoing U.S. ballistic missile defense program will have a direct impact on force developments in Asia. As the United States proceeds with its program, without question, China will insist on maintaining its deterrent force at levels necessary to compensate for the U.S. program. The extent of China's nuclear modernization, in both quantity and quality, can and will be determined by what the Chinese see the United States doing. If U.S. actions, as well as U.S. statements, make it clear that there is no need for the Chinese to overreact for reasons of their national security, this would be the best outcome for all concerned.

China thus far has been content with a modest force of long-range strategic weapons—far less than most predictions of a larger buildup dating back more than thirty years. But China's technical and industrial ability and national commitment to maintain a retaliatory capability at higher levels, if necessary, is not in doubt.

The United States should engage China in a dialogue through a Consultative Group for Strategic Security created for this purpose, similar to the group established by the Bush-Putin Declaration of Moscow. This U.S.-China group should address issues important to both, such as confidence-building, improving transparency and stability, strengthening early warning against accidental missile launch, and enhancing stability in the Asia-Pacific region. Engaging with China in this fashion should provide a better basis for U.S. program decisions. China's decision-making also could be better informed through this process, especially if it included sound technical judgments that avoided exaggerated performance claims about the proposed ballistic missile defense systems.

North Korea

Anti-proliferation policies pursued in the past in the case of North Korea (DPRK) have emphasized denial but also incentives. The so-called "Perry process," an effort led by William Perry, former secretary of defense during the Clinton administration, was an example of this, as was the 1994 U.S.–North Korea Agreed Framework. Coercive diplomacy, including the threat of force and application of sanctions, also has been tried. These policies have succeeded in slowing North Korea's nuclear weapons and ballistic missile programs but not in stopping them.

North Korea illustrates the limited utility of force in rolling back nascent nuclear weapons capabilities. If hostilities occurred, North Korean military forces massed just north of the Demilitarized Zone between North and South Korea could inflict massive damage on Seoul, the largest population center of South Korea. In addition, popular opinion in South Korea has turned against the idea that force should be used to destroy North Korea's nuclear potential. Fear of U.S. military power no doubt influences North Korea's actions and will continue to do so. An element of coercion, backed by U.S. military force, will inevitably be a part of the U.S.-DPRK equation. But it is not likely to be sufficient to stop North Korea's nuclear programs.

The 1994 U.S.-DPRK Agreed Framework acknowledged that a broad political and economic program of cooperation would be necessary to dismantle, conclusively, North Korea's nuclear weapons program. That broader program lacked political support in the United States, and North Korean behavior was not helpful. The launch of a ballistic missile over Japan in 1998 did not exactly spur on North Korea's partners to implement the Agreed Framework. And so the program was not fully implemented. At some point in time, the North Korean leadership decided to hedge its bets and to open up an alternative route to a nuclear weapons capability in violation of the 1994 Agreed Framework.

North Korea has come closer to acquiring a robust arsenal of nuclear weapons than any of the other potential proliferants. But the lessons of previous anti-proliferation efforts in North Korea, and elsewhere, suggest that the best hope of stopping North Korea's nuclear weapons programs lies in a broad settlement of long-festering problems in and around the Korean peninsula, rather than in a narrow focus just on North Korea's nuclear programs.

As one step in targeted diplomacy in halting North Korea's nuclear programs, it may be necessary to negotiate a non-use of force commitment between the United States and North Korea in the context of a freeze and dismantlement of all North Korea's nuclear weapons programs. Reinstatement of the obligations of the Agreed Framework would be accompanied by the return of IAEA inspectors with the authority to inspect the elements of a gas centrifuge facility that North Korea has acquired. At some early point, the issue of removing the plutonium, including all spent fuel rods, from North Korea must be addressed, and North Korea's nuclear weapons facilities and program dismantled.

It would be a serious mistake to allow the process to stop there. The North Korean leadership is primarily interested in survival and seems to be aware that economic changes will be necessary for that to happen. Unless the leadership becomes firmly committed to that route and convinced that it will be safe to pursue it—or the present government collapses under the weight of its domestic failures and abuses—the leadership will persist in its development of a nuclear weapons capability. Crisis will follow crisis until military action or acceptance of North Korea as a nuclear weapon state are the only alternatives.

The Bush administration has called for a multilateral discussion of the security issues pertaining to North Korea and its environs. This approach makes sense. It provides the multilateral context that is all-important to anti-proliferation policies. In the North Korean case, a broad program of economic cooperation involving North Korea must proceed on a multilateral basis. And security guarantees should ultimately include North Korea's neighbors— South Korea, above all. Since North Korea poses a threat to its neighbors, guarantees must be a two-way street.

Some issues probably can only be resolved through trilateral talks between the United States and South and North Korea aimed at revising the system created by the armistice agreement of 1953. Most likely Russia, China, and Japan will also play a prominent role in the diplomatic steps leading to a peace treaty and to other obligations undertaken among the parties, although not all the obligations will be of concern to every party. A new basis for a U.S. military presence in the Korean peninsula may also need to be devised, one perhaps modeled on NATO's "Partnership for Peace." Other nations should also be included in a new security mechanism for Northeast Asia. The Shanghai Cooperation Organization could be a model for this.

This book is not the place for detailed discussion of these elements of a settlement. The point here is that the goal of non-proliferation can be achieved in Northeast Asia but that it must be part of a broader and more multilateral process than in the past. Each of the longer-term items in the Agreed Framework relating to the normalization of relationships between the United States and North Korea needs to be reviewed to determine whether specific dates for implementation are possible. And they should be placed squarely in an ongoing multilateral peace process in Northeast Asia.

Are the U.S. Congress and the American public ready for this? With presidential leadership, perhaps so, especially since the alternative very likely will be not only a nuclear-armed North Korea but also the entry of Japan and South Korea into the ranks of nuclear-weapon states. This would affect China, which would affect India, which would affect Pakistan. An Asian arms race rivaling the

Cold War's U.S.-Soviet nuclear arms race could be the result.

Iran

Iran is positioning itself to become a nuclear weapon state by developing the essential infrastructure, including skilled technical people. The American response has been to rely on denial policies. So far, those efforts have not succeeded in blocking Iran's programs. Russia, despite heavy U.S. pressure, has continued to assist Iran's nuclear power programs, arguing that Iran is entitled to this under the nuclear Non-Proliferation Treaty and that, with enforcement of IAEA provisions for verification, Russia does not envisage a nuclear weapons threat arising in Iran. Recently Russia has begun to press Iran to accept the IAEA Additional Protocol. In the background of this controversy are Russia's interest in building influence with an important neighbor, its interest in strengthening its own economy, and its perception that it too often has been cut out of civilian nuclear power programs. The self-serving hand of MINATOM is also evident.

Unlike the case of the nuclear weapons program in North Korea, there is no evidence that Iran has acquired the nuclear material necessary to build a bomb. The evidence suggests that it will be a few years before Iran will be in a position to fabricate a nuclear weapon unless it succeeds in acquiring the material from another nation. With time available to head off Iran's becoming a nuclear weapon state, the exercise of targeted diplomacy is in order. It should involve a multilateral effort, as in the case of North Korea, not just a U.S. campaign.

Any analysis of Iran's possible motivations in acquiring nuclear weapons would probably conclude that the country has real security problems, which nuclear weapons might address, and that national prestige might also be a factor. And again in contrast to North Korea, it is possible that Iran's leadership has not made up its collective mind about acquiring nuclear weapons, even though the infrastructure is being carefully put in place.

Incontrovertibly, Iran lives in a dangerous neighborhood. To its north is Russia, a country with which Iran once had territorial disputes and with which it still has disputes concerning oil in the Caspian Sea. To its east is nuclear-armed, and unstable, Pakistan. Pakistan's nuclear arsenal may very well be influencing thinking in Tehran regarding nuclear weapons. Also in the east, a highly volatile Afghanistan still sunk in the mire of warlordism is far from reassuring. To Iran's south lies Saudi Arabia, potentially due for internal change with an uncertain outcome, and sponsor of Wahhabism, a very different form of Islam from that practiced in Iran. And to its west is Iraq, with whom Iran fought a bitter eight-year war, whose dictator, Saddam Hussein, was well on the way to acquiring nuclear weapons, and whose influence probably is still felt in Tehran. Farther afield is nuclear-armed Israel, victim of Iran-sponsored terrorism, and therefore no friend. And across the sea lies the "Great Satan," the United States, considered by the conservative Iranian leadership to be the archenemy. And, of course, the United States is the preeminent nuclear weapon state. Beyond all this, Iran sees itself as a major regional power which, in itself, creates a certain demand for advanced weaponry.

What could targeted diplomacy do about such a messy

situation? How could Iran's legitimate security concerns, which presumably are driving its interest in nuclear technology, be alleviated? Some things were done which should be a relief to Iran but which will also generate additional security concerns. Those were the Bush administration's removal of the Taliban from power in Afghanistan, and its campaign to unseat Saddam Hussein and end Iraq's nuclear aspirations. The successful conclusion of that campaign has eliminated a major source of Iran's security concerns. But now, instead of a hostile and ambitious Saddam Hussein, Iran sees the "Great Satan" on its doorstep, in the west as in the east. It sees powerful American forces poised to deal with the next member of Bush's "axis of evil." There is talk already of "marching on Tehran" and charges that Iran is aiding Al Qaeda and the Taliban and meddling in Iraq. The need to acquire nuclear weapons may appear in the minds of Iran's leaders to be more urgent than ever.

But Iran is another example of a nation where a U.S. preventive or preemptive military attack would be highly unlikely. There is little likelihood that support would be extended from any quarter to the United States if it contemplated such an attack. Instead, the reaction of America's friends and allies, Russia, Turkey, Saudi Arabia, and Pakistan, would almost certainly be hostile. The reaction in Western Europe would be negative and would deny the United States the support it needs to achieve its broader goals in the Middle East. Here again is a case where a nuclear proliferation problem has to be addressed in the context of accommodating the strategic interests of the United States, of the potential proliferant, and of the neighboring states.

How to achieve this? The most immediate need would be to reassure Iran that U.S. forces in the Middle East can serve Iran's interests. It will be impossible to realize the possible benefits of a U.S. troop presence in the Middle East unless U.S. policy toward Iran is radically changed, and, correspondingly, Iran's policy in support of terrorists. Iran's influence with Iraq's Shiites, of course, also will affect the prospects for a rapprochement. Given some good-faith moves on the part of the Tehran government, the United States should temper its "axis of evil" rhetoric and work to reestablish its links with that government while continuing to support democratic factions—not an easy task. Otherwise, U.S. objectives in the Middle East, including its anti-proliferation objectives, will not be realized.

In return, Iran, which has accepted IAEA safeguards, should be obligated to accept the Additional Protocol discussed earlier, which would strengthen IAEA authority to carry out challenge inspection of suspect facilities. Russia and Britain are pushing Iran hard on this issue. Iran should renounce any plans to reprocess spent fuel rods to acquire weapons-grade plutonium. Iran also should abandon its uranium enrichment program. If this is done, the United States should be willing to provide technical assistance in the energy field to Iran.

At some point in the next several years, security ties with Iran should be developed, including arms sales as compensation for forgoing nuclear programs. Iran, of course, must also take steps to make that politically possible for the United States. And that means that Iran must finally drop any support for terrorist activities. In that context, U.S. sanctions regarding many aspects of trade with

Iran also would be dropped, though embargoes relating to their ability to develop nuclear weapons would be maintained.

All this probably would prove to be insufficient to convince Iran to forgo a nuclear weapons capability if the United States alone were Iran's negotiating partner. But this does not appear to be the case, and coalition diplomacy has now come into play in order to convince Iran that it will have no support in its quest for nuclear weapons.

A second step to move Iran away from its present course would be to involve Israel in this effort. Israel's evident status as an undeclared nuclear weapon state probably is one of the factors motivating Iran in this direction. The changes in Iraq and the political changes within the Palestinian Authority may make it possible for Israel to return to some ideas it has entertained in the past. An Israeli-backed proposal for a nuclear weapons–free zone in the Middle East, to be monitored by a strengthened International Atomic Energy Agency, and guaranteed by the United States, might be a decisive step in persuading Iran not to become a nuclear weapon state. But this will inevitably await progress in resolving the Israeli-Palestinian conflict.

The Bush administration hopes that the overthrow of Saddam Hussein's regime will lead to the spread of democracy in the Middle East. Maybe it will, but Western-style democracy will be a long time in coming to all, or even most, of the states of the region. A more realizable, shorter-term goal would be to use the altered circumstances in the Middle East to reverse the trend toward nuclear proliferation, there and elsewhere. Iran, under the control of the conservative clergy, will resist this but democratic change seems to be on the way. When that develops more fully, a more creative U.S. policy toward Iran could make a big difference.

Israel

Israel has never acknowledged acquiring nuclear weapons, but the general assumption is that it has built a substantial stockpile of them as its ultimate defense against hostile neighbors with populations greatly outnumbering its own, and replete with organizations that deny its right to exist. In any event, the existence of such a stockpile is accepted by governments in the Middle East as a fact and their policies are based on that proposition. The interest shown by Iraq and Iran in acquiring nuclear weapons partly derives from that assessment, as well as from their sporadic ambitions for regional dominance and their hostility toward each other. The quest to block the spread of nuclear weapons in the Middle East will never be completely successful until the Israeli nuclear weapons capability is addressed in a way that satisfies the perceived security and political needs of both Israel and its neighbors.

As in every other known case of nuclear proliferation, decisions by Middle Eastern countries to build nuclear weapons cannot be divorced from the strategic context in which the motivation to acquire them was formed. In Israel's case the hostility shown by most Arab states obviously was the motivating factor, reinforced by the experience of war and terrorism.

A truce in the Israeli-Palestinian conflict, and its resolution along the lines of the two-state model being pressed by the Bush administration, is an absolute requirement for a successful U.S. anti-proliferation program in the Middle East. American national interests require vigorous prosecution of the "road map" project sponsored by the United States and several other governments, which is designed to lead to the establishment, within a relatively brief time-span, of a Palestinian state.

Absent real progress on this front, the problem of nuclear weapons will not be settled in the Middle East, and repeated "preventive" military actions will be deemed necessary, either by Israel or by the United States. The problem will not end with the departure of Saddam Hussein from the stage. The new security situation created in the Middle East by the intervention of U.S. military forces in Iraq presents all the major actors in Middle Eastern politics with an unparalleled opportunity to resolve the nuclear dilemma, or at least to begin negotiations to achieve that goal.

This is a good time to begin raising the question of eliminating all nuclear weapons from the Middle East, in the aftermath of the Saddam Hussein era, while the United States has a strong presence in the area, and while talks are under way with the new government of the Palestinian Authority to implement the road map presented to Israel and the Palestinians. Raising the nuclear issue would not be a distraction. Instead, it would help create a more positive environment from which Israel would benefit.

If it is to consider joining in discussions about a nuclear-free Middle East, Israel would require a credible security guarantee from the United States. In the context of a broad settlement of the Israeli-Palestinian conflict, it should receive one. The Palestinian Authority may ask for NATO or U.S. peacekeeping troops to oversee a settlement of the border and other elements of a settlement. This approach deserves and needs serious consideration.

If these things come to pass, it is not so inconceivable that Israel would agree to a nuclear-free Middle East. Previous Israeli governments have been ready to think about this concept, so it is not a new and radical idea. Furthermore, UN Security Council Resolution 687, adopted in 1991, contains a recommendation that the goal should be a zone free of weapons of mass destruction in the Middle East. This would lead to a verified abandonment of all nuclear ambitions by all of Israel's neighbors, including Iran, if given appropriate security assurances. The key to this, however, would be the continuing strong support of Israeli security by the United States, and not just promises given by other nations to remain non-nuclear.

Is this utopian? Not when the enormous seismic shock of the U.S. action in Iraq is fully recognized. Not if the interests of the Arab states and Iran are taken into account in a broad settlement of issues preventing peace in the Middle East. And certainly not in comparison with the concept of remaking all of the Middle East to conform to the democratic image that President Bush has said is his goal. In the end, this kind of settlement would be the best consequence of the huge risks taken by the Bush administration in the Iraqi intervention.

India and Pakistan

Rollback, in the case of India and Pakistan, is not likely to be achieved short of major changes in their relationships with each other. Furthermore, given India's justifiable claim to a global power status, significant changes probably would have to be effected in nuclear relations among the declared nuclear weapon states in order for India to renounce nuclear weapons.

But India and Pakistan could become partners of the United States in an anti-proliferation campaign. It is not too late for that. At the moment, it appears that the two countries have not deployed ballistic missiles mated with nuclear warheads. In some respects, their nuclear weapons have not been completely operationalized. There is still ample scope for arranging their nuclear forces and their policies in a way that would contribute to the rollback policy advocated in this book.

What would have to be done? First, both India and Pakistan should publicly and unequivocally uphold all of the non-transfer provisions of the NPT. They should also hew rigorously to the Nuclear Suppliers Group guidelines and, in addition, support enhanced monitoring capabilities for the IAEA. Since missile technology is also a critical factor in relations between them and other nations, each nation should accept the restrictions of the Missile Technology Control Regime.

Second, they should cap their nuclear weapons development programs where they now are. No further nuclear test explosions should be conducted. Ideally, they should both adhere to the CTBT, but U.S. ratification will be the minimum necessary to achieve that, and even that may not be enough. Actions to make the current nuclear test moratorium more stable and verifiable, as suggested earlier, should be pursued with both countries.

Third, they should implement the Lahore Declaration

issued on February 21, 1999, by Prime Minister Vajpayee of India and then prime minister Sharif of Pakistan. It was an important statement of intent, which could still be a useful basis for reducing tension and enhancing cooperation between the two countries. Unfortunately, India and Pakistan entered yet another of their periodic military crises before much could be done to implement the declaration. All of the confidence-building measures described in the Lahore Declaration should be put into effect without delay. They deal with notifications of ballistic missile flight tests, measures to reduce the risks of accidental or unauthorized use of nuclear weapons, continuing their moratorium on nuclear test explosions, preventing incidents at sea, upgrading communications links, and establishing consultative mechanisms. Such measures are even more essential when tensions are running high between the two countries.

And fourth, India and Pakistan should offer to join in regional stability arrangements with China. This could include transparency and confidence-building measures, cooperation in early warning, measures to avoid hair-trigger launch status for ballistic missiles, and, perhaps, agreements regarding ceilings on nuclear force levels

The argument of this book is that non-proliferation objectives are best attained in a context that recognizes the broad strategic interests of the countries involved, and in a multilateral framework. This presumes that the United States will press for a serious anti-proliferation policy, including rollback or scale-back of nuclear weapons. The current Bush administration has been willing to keep the nuclear weapons issue off the table so long as India and Pakistan do nothing to put it there. That has satisfied all parties for the moment but it leaves the future very uncertain.

The Bush administration's interest in having Pakistan and India join the United States as partners in the fight against international terrorism has led to support for them in material ways. This has met some of the security concerns and some of the status questions of the two countries, and the United States should continue to work with them to enhance their security and their economic development. The element of strategic nuclear restraint must play an important part in the relationships sooner rather than later. President Bush reportedly has pressed Pakistan's President Musharraf very hard regarding Pakistan's support for North Korea's nuclear program. Neither American nor Indian nor Pakistani interests would be served by actions that stimulated a nuclear arms race in Asia. None of them would benefit from actions that made it easier for other potential proliferants to acquire nuclear weapons. These considerations should become a stronger element in the U.S.-Pakistani-Indian agenda.

To encourage such policies, the United States should offer to help in constructing an early warning system in South Asia, linking it to China, if possible. The United States should consider inviting China, Pakistan, and India to participate with it in air-and-missile defense cooperation. As recommended above, the United States should also work to reduce the salience of nuclear weapons in its own defense policies, which might influence China, and thus India, and thus Pakistan, as well.

Effective safety, security, and command and control arrangements for Indian and Pakistani nuclear weapons within a regime of nuclear restraint are as important to the United States as they are to India and Pakistan. They would lessen the risk of accidental or unauthorized attacks that could escalate into destabilizing regional conflict damaging to U.S. interests. The United States should include these issues in the broad nuclear agenda suggested above, and not separately from it.

The United States should not recognize India and Pakistan as de jure nuclear weapon states. This would do great damage, perhaps fatal harm, to the NPT. Would tacit recognition of India and Pakistan as de facto nuclear weapon states by the United States weaken the NPT and the regime surrounding it? It is a clear and important U.S. interest that India and Pakistan commit themselves to the anti-proliferation program recommended above. This would involve a more overt U.S. acceptance of India and Pakistan as de facto nuclear weapon states than ever before. It is worth the price.

VII. Conclusion

THE CHALLENGE FACED by the international community today is to meet new threats to the non-proliferation regime with all the inspiration and determination it can muster. In the past this effort has achieved considerable success; and furthermore there is no desirable alternative to this. By its very nature an effort to sustain and strengthen the non-proliferation regime requires world-wide cooperation and strong leadership by the United States. To make progress toward this goal it will be essential to call on all the tools of diplomacy balanced with credible military strength and exercised with patience and determination.

A Call to Action

1. The United States must wage a determined, long-term campaign against nuclear proliferation. Victory in this campaign is essential for the security of this nation and all other nations in the world. Defeat in this struggle would endanger civilization.

2. This campaign should be directed at containing and rolling back the number of nuclear weapon states. The United States and its friends already have achieved an encouraging record of success in creating and maintaining a non-proliferation regime that has limited the spread of nuclear weapons to eight declared, undeclared, and de facto nuclear powers. A powerful norm of non-possession

and non-use of nuclear weapons was built up throughout the darkest years of the Cold War. This record gives confidence that the United States can do as well today despite new dangers arising at what President Bush has called the "crossroads of technology and radicalism."

3. By its actions the United States must reinforce a fundamental consensus that nuclear weapons are weapons of last resort, deployed to deter nuclear attack, and to retaliate accordingly if that fails. This implies reciprocally reducing with Russia reliance on nuclear weapons, and scaling back their numbers. Developing new and purportedly more usable ones for limited missions would undercut achieving this goal.

4. The United States should recognize and rely heavily on the power of diplomacy, backed by all the elements of national power and exercised with patience and determination, in its efforts to prevent the proliferation of nuclear weapons. The use of force and of denial policies play important roles but cannot do the whole job, or even a large part of it. There is a historical precedent for preemptive action, but international agreement on what constitutes appropriate preventive actions has yet to be established. To be effective, diplomacy must broadly address basic motivations of would-be proliferant nations, and be targeted to meet their individual concerns about their national security, prestige, and economies. Focusing solely on the goal of anti-proliferation itself is inadequate.

5. The United States must engage in and strongly support specific actions that can serve as effective instruments in the effort against proliferation. These include giving strong support to the Nunn-Lugar Cooperative Threat Reduction Program; strengthening the nuclear Non-Pro-

liferation Treaty and expanding the authority of the International Atomic Energy Agency for on-site inspections of suspicious activities; continuing the moratorium on underground nuclear explosive testing while addressing the important task of ratifying the Comprehensive Test Ban Treaty and leading a worldwide effort to bring it into force; and pursuing multilateral cooperation on defensive and early warning systems that can help build a stronger anti-proliferation coalition and reduce nuclear danger.

About the Authors

SIDNEY D. DRELL is professor of physics emeritus at Stanford University's Linear Accelerator Center and a senior fellow at its Hoover Institution. For many years he has been an adviser to the U.S. government on technical national security and arms control issues, including membership on the President's Foreign Intelligence Advisory Board and Science Advisory Committee. His writings on nuclear weapons include "In the Shadow of the Bomb" (American Institute of Physics, 1993) and "Reducing Nuclear Danger" (with McGeorge Bundy and William Crowe, Council on Foreign Relations, 1993). Honors recognizing his contributions to both physics and national security include the Enrico Fermi Medal, the National Intelligence Distinguished Service Medal, a MacArthur Fellowship, and election to the National Academy of Sciences.

JAMES E. GOODBY served as a career diplomat, holding a number of ambassadorial-rank positions, several concerning nuclear weapons issues. After leaving the U.S. Foreign Service, he taught at Carnegie Mellon, Georgetown, and Stanford and wrote or edited several books and many articles on national security issues. Currently, he is associated with the Center for Northeast Asian Policy Studies at the Brookings Institution and the Securities Studies Program at MIT. He co-authored this book while a diplomat-in-residence at Stanford's Institute for International Studies. He is the winner of the Heinz Award in Public Policy, the Commander's Cross of the Order of Merit of Germany, and the Presidential Distinguished Service Award and the holder of an honorary Doctor of Laws from the Stetson University College of Law.

Index

ABM Treaty. *See* Anti-Ballistic
Missile (ABM) Treaty
Afghanistan, 111, 112
Africa, 37, 40
Al Qaeda, 112
Albright, David, 56
Annan, Kofi, 27
Anti-Ballistic Missile (ABM) Treaty,
58–59
anti-proliferation, Bush, George H.
W., enforcement of, 13, 47–48; Call
to Action for, 122–24; consensus,
3, 47, 123; economical benefits
from, 76; funding, 85–86; IAEA
support of, 2; monitoring problems
for, 53–58; new regime
development for, 3, 47, 95–97;
policies, vii–viii, 2, 7–10, 73;
preemptive considerations for, 34–
38; success of, 87; United States
leadership of, viii, 3, 5, 7–10, 30–
31, 63–64; withdrawal, 2–3
Argentina, 37, 40
Asia. *See* China; Japan; North Korea;
South Korea

Baker, Howard, 84, 86
Baker, James, 67
ballistic missile defense, 8, 10; in
China, 104–5; denial policies and,
58–61; Europe-oriented, 82; export
control of, 60; impact of, 59–60; in
India, 119; intercontinental, 79,
104; international cooperation for,
60–61, 82–83; in Pakistan, 53, 119;
stability of, 79–80; United States
support of, 58–59
Belarus, 14, 37, 40
Berlin, 19, 25

Bilateral Implementation
Commission, 80
biological weapons, Iraqi use of, 67–
68; nuclear weapons *v.*, 1, 70;
technical factors of, 17–18; U.S. use
of, 16
Blair, Tony, 35
Blix, Hans, 98
bombs. *See specific types of bombs*
borders, security of, 29, 45
Brazil, 37, 40
"bunker busters," 17, 69–70
Bush, George H. W., 13, 47–48, 67
Bush, George W., Iraq war
assessment by, 42, 67–68; Moscow
Declaration by Putin and, 9, 77–78;
9/11 assessment by, 35; NPT
compliance improvements by, 87;
nuclear weapons assessment by,
vii, 1, 35–36; Pakistani support
requested by, 120
Bush-Putin Declaration (Moscow), 9,
77–78, 82–83, 87, 106

Canada, funding from, 86
Carter, Jimmy, 12, 37
Caspian Sea, oil disputes over, 111
Central Asian Nuclear Free Zone, 76
centrifuge systems, for gas, 52; for
uranium, 51
cesium 137, 46
CGSS. *See* Consultative Group for
Strategic Security
Chelyabinsk, 100
chemical weapons, 17; in Iraq, 67–
68; nuclear weapons *v.*, 1, 70
China, ballistic missiles in, 104–5;
CGSS involvement by, 106;
Consultative Commission for, 9;